REVISE EDEXCEL GCSE (9–1)
English Language
GUIDED REVISION WORKBOOK

Series Consultant: Harry Smith

Author: Eileen Sagar

Also available to support your revision:

Revise GCSE Study Skills Guide   9781447967071

The **Revise GCSE Study Skills Guide** is full of tried-and-trusted hints and tips for how to learn more effectively. It gives you techniques to help you achieve your best – throughout your GCSE studies and beyond!

Revise GCSE Revision Planner   9781447967828

The **Revise GCSE Revision Planner** helps you to plan and organise your time, step-by-step, throughout your GCSE revision. Use this book and wall chart to mastermind your revision.

REVISE GCSE
Study Skills
GUIDE

REVISE GCSE
REVISION PLANNER

For the full range of Pearson revision titles across KS2, KS3, GCSE, Functional Skills, AS/A Level and BTEC visit: www.pearsonschools.co.uk/revise

Pearson

Contents

A small bit of small print

Edexcel publishes Sample Assessment Material and the Specification on its website. This is the official content and this book should be used in conjunction with it. The questions in this book have been written to help you practise what you have learned in your revision. Remember: the real exam questions may not look like this.

Planning your exam time

It is important to use your time wisely in the exam. Look closely at the examples of exam-style questions below. **You don't need to answer these questions.** Instead, look at the marks and think about how long you should spend answering each type of question.

> For Paper 1, there are four questions in Section A – Reading. You should spend about an hour on this section.

Paper

①

me allowed:
hour and
5 minutes

1 From lines 1–3, identify a phrase which explains why the mayor would expect others to obey him.   **(1 mark)**

3 In lines 16–21, how does the writer use language and structure to suggest that the mayor is successful?
Support your views with reference to the text.   **(6 marks)**

> For Paper 2, there are seven questions. Questions 1–3 are for Text 1. Questions 4–6 are for Text 2. Question 7 is in two parts: (a) and (b). They require you to refer to both texts in your answers. You must answer both sections of the question.

Paper
②

me allowed:
2 hours

1 In lines 14–16, identify **two** things the adult world does not owe teenagers.   **(2 marks)**

6 The writer attempts to engage the reader with the argument that fidget spinners are not a good idea. Evaluate how successfully this is achieved.
Support your views with detailed reference to the text.   **(15 marks)**

7 **(a)** The two texts are both about teenagers.
What similarities are there in the attitudes to teenagers?
Use evidence from both texts to support your answer.   **(6 marks)**

1 How many minutes should you spend reading the source texts and questions before you start each exam?

Paper 1: 10 minutes. Paper 2: ....

2 Roughly how many minutes should you spend on Paper 1, Question 1?

....

3 What part of the extract should you refer to in your answer to Paper 1, Question 1?

You should refer to lines...................................

4 How many minutes should you spend on Paper 2, Question 6?

....

5 How many texts should you use to answer Paper 2, Question 7 (a)?

....

6 Which of the following should you do before you start to answer any questions? Circle your choices:

- Read all the questions.
- Skim read the source texts to identify the main ideas and themes.
- Highlight or annotate relevant information in the texts.
- Read the texts a second time.
- Notice how many marks are awarded and work out how much time to spend on each question.

Reading texts explained

Read this short extract from *Wuthering Heights* and answer Question 1 below. This is preparation, you won't get a question like this in the exam. Part (a) has been done for you.

> When you read any text, think about:
> • how and why the author has created certain characters/atmospheres
> • the writer's purpose, tone and point of view.

> So, from the very beginning, he bred <u>bad feeling</u> in the house; and at Mrs Earnshaw's death, which happened in less than two years after, the young master had learnt to regard his father as an <u>oppressor</u> rather than a friend, and Heathcliff as a <u>usurper of his father's affections</u> and his privileges, and he grew <u>bitter with brooding</u> over these injuries.

1 (a) Underline words or phrases which you think create an impression of life in the house.

(b) What impression of life in the house do you think is created here?

The words suggest that the people in the house are troubled and uneasy. The words

....

....

....

....

> Read as much and as widely as you can outside of lesson time. This will help you to think about how writers create atmosphere and character.

Now read this short extract from *I am Malala*, then answer Question 2 below. This is preparation, not an exam-style question.

2 Underline the words or phrases in the extract that show the writer's point of view about her move to Birmingham. Two have been done for you. Then use the sentence openers to complete the annotations.

> The words 'plucked' and 'transported' give the impression that the narrator's move from Swat to Birmingham was unexpected. Malala's life............
>
> ....
>
> ....

Despite the
upheaval of moving,

....

....

....

....

....

> My family has been through many changes. We were <u>plucked</u> from our mountain valley in Swat, Pakistan, and <u>transported</u> to a brick house in Birmingham, England's second-biggest city. Sometimes it seems so strange to me that I want to pinch myself. I'm 17 now and one thing that has not changed is that I still don't like getting up in the morning. The most astonishing thing is that it's my father whose voice wakes me up now. He gets up first every day and prepares breakfast for me, my mother and my brothers Atal and Khushal.

From 'mountain
valley' to 'brick
house' suggests

....

....

....

....

....

Reading questions explained 1

There are four assessment objectives in Section A Reading: Assessment objective 1 (AO1),
Assessment objective 2 (AO2), Assessment objective 3 (AO3) and Assessment objective 4 (AO4).
Read AO1 and AO2 below.

Assessment objective 1
(a) Identify and interpret explicit and implicit
    information and ideas
(b) Select and synthesise evidence from
    different texts

Assessment objective 2
Explain, comment on and analyse how
writers use language and structure to achieve
effects and influence readers, using relevant
subject terminology to support their views

Assessment objective 3
Compare writers' ideas and perspectives, as well as how these are conveyed, across two or more texts

Look at the following exam-style questions. **You don't need to answer these questions.**
Instead, identify the assessment objective (or the part of the assessment objective) that is being
tested and circle it.

Paper ①

1 From line 19–23, identify the phrase which suggests that Susan expected her husband
   to be in a different situation from the one she is witnessing at this point in the story.   **(1 mark)**

  1 The question above tests: AO1(a) AO1(b) AO2 AO3

Paper ①

2 From lines 25–31, give **two** reasons why Susan might be affected by seeing her
   husband again.
   You may use your own words or quotation from the text.   **(6 marks)**

> The words 'give' and 'identify' in questions 1 and 2
> mean that you are not required to go into detail.

  2 The question above tests: AO1(a) AO1(b) AO2 AO3

Paper ②

7 (a) The two texts are about the need to take action.
        What similarities do both texts share when it comes to taking action?
        Use evidence from both texts to support your answer.   **(6 marks)**

  3 The question above tests: AO1(a) AO1(b) AO2 AO3

> To get the highest marks for AO3, you will need to demonstrate your ability to
> compare writers' ideas and perspectives across the two different texts provided
> in the question paper. You will need to refer to differences, as well as similarities.

Paper ②

7 (b) Compare how the writers of 'Freedom or death' and 'Wayward plastic' present their ideas
        and perspectives on how people should take action.
        Support your answer with detailed reference to the text.   **(14 marks)**

  4 The question above tests: AO1(a) AO1(b) AO2 AO3

Reading questions explained 2

Read the description of AO4 and the example exam-style questions below. Then answer the question.

Assessment objective 4
Evaluate texts critically and support this with appropriate textual references

> Question 4 on Paper 1 (fiction) and Question 6 on Paper 2 (non-fiction) assess AO4. Both questions carry 15 marks each, so it is important that you practise the skills needed to answer AO4 questions.

Paper ①

4 In this extract, there is an attempt to show humour when the narrator has to account for his visit to Miss Havisham.
Evaluate how successfully this is achieved.
Support your views with detailed reference to the text. **(15 marks)**

Paper ②

6 Bill Bryson attempts to engage the reader by using an entertaining description of his arrival at the hotel.
Evaluate how successfully this is achieved.
Support your views with detailed reference to the text. **(15 marks)**

> Look at how each question is worded. In both, the phrase 'attempts to' is used in relation to the writer. For the fiction you will be writing about how the writer 'shows' a theme (for example, humour). For the non-fiction you will be looking at how the writer 'engages' the reader. For both questions, you are asked to 'evaluate how successfully this is achieved' and 'support your views'.

Guided

Read the extract from *Great Expectations* on page 96 and *Notes from a Small Island* on page 102. Then choose one of the exam-style questions above and make a plan of what you might want to use in your answer. Make notes on:

- the points you want to make
- a range of examples from the text (quotations and textual references)
- how successfully the writer achieves what he has set out to do.

> This is not another language and structure question. You should write about SITE elements of the texts (settings, ideas, themes and/or events).

....

....

....

....

....

....

....

....

....

....

> **Remember:** You will be given more space in the exam to write your answer in full.

Reading the questions

Read the exam-style question below. **You don't need to answer this question.**
Instead, think about what it is asking you to do and answer the questions that follow.

Paper ① **2** From lines <u>6–11</u>, give **two** reasons why <u>Miss Dean preferred looking after Heathcliff</u>. You may use your own words or quotations from the text. **(2 marks)**

1 (a) Highlight or underline:
- the part of the extract you are being asked to use for your answer
- how many pieces of information you are being asked to find
- the focus of the question.

(b) Which word in the question above, shows you only need to **find** reasons, rather than provide a full explanation for each one?

....

2 Look at the exam-style questions below. **You don't need to answer this question.**
Instead, annotate each question to show the following information:
- how many texts you need to write about
- how much of each text you should use for your answer
- the key words in the question
- how long you should spend on your answer.

Paper ① **3** In lines 19–29, how does the writer use language and structure to show Heathcliff's behaviour and attitude?
Support your views with reference to the text. **(6 marks)**

Paper ② **6** Malala Yousafza attempts to make the reader understand how the family felt when they first arrived from Swat to begin a new life in England.
Evaluate how successfully this is achieved.
Support your views with detailed reference to the text. **(15 marks)**

Paper ② **7** (a) The two texts describe the ways women's lives need to change. What similarities are there in the changes suggested in the texts?
Use evidence from both texts to support your answer. **(6 marks)**

Skimming for the main idea or theme

Look at this short extract from 'Are fidget spinners a scam?' from the *Daily Mail Online*, then answer the questions below.

> **Are fidget spinners a scam? Researchers say there is no proof the hit toys help people with ADHD and autism**
> • Fidget spinners are small devices that a person can spin between his/her fingers
> • They're being sold everywhere from internet retailer to street vendor and stores
> • The device has even been marketed as an aide for ADHD, autism and anxiety, however no formal academic studies on their effect have been conducted

1 (a) What does the headline suggest about the main idea or theme of the article?

The headline suggests that the main theme of the article is whether or not fidget spinners are a con.

(b) What does the closing sentence suggest about the main idea or theme of the article?

The closing sentence suggests ....

....

Now read the next three paragraphs from the full article on page 101 (lines 7–13) then answer the questions below.

2 (a) What does this section of the article suggest about the article's main theme?

It suggests that the article is showing ....

....

....

(b) Do the ideas expressed in this section of the article differ from those you found at the beginning?

At the beginning of the article ....

....

> Skim reading a text can give you a good idea of what it is about before you read it more closely. Look at:
> • the headline, title or headings   • the last sentence of the text.   • the first sentence of each paragraph

Now skim read the whole article on page 101 for 30 seconds, then answer Question 3.

3 (a) Write four bullet points that sum up the main idea in the article as a whole:

• Fidget spinners are popular   • ....

• ....   • ....

(b) Rewrite your bullet points as one or two sentences.

....

....

(c) Now rewrite your sentences again, improving them.

....

....

Annotating the texts

Read this extract from *Great Expectations*. It has been annotated by a student.

'That's true, Mum,' said Mr Pumblechook, <u>with a grave nod</u>. 'That's the state of the case, for that much I've seen myself. And then they both stared at me, and I, with an <u>obtrusive[4] show of artlessness[5]</u> on my <u>countenance[6]</u>, stared at them, and <u>plaited[7] the right leg of my trousers with my right hand</u>.
<u>If they had asked me any more questions I should <u>undoubtedly have betrayed</u> myself, for I was even then on the point of mentioning that there was a balloon in the yard, and should have hazarded[8] the statement but for <u>my invention being divided</u> between that phenomenon and a bear in the brewery[9]. They were so much occupied, however, in discussing the marvels I had already presented for their consideration, that I escaped.

4: *obtrusive* – noticeable
5: *artlessness* – lack of deception
6: *countenance* – facial expression

7: *plaited* – pleated or folded over
8: *hazarded* – guessed without confidence
9: *brewery* – a place where beer is made

A Reference to 'plaited' suggests that the narrator is playing with the cloth out of nerves.

B Adjective 'obtrusive' suggests the narrator makes his lies look convincing through facial expression.

C Phrase 'undoubtedly have betrayed' suggests his outrageous lies would have given him away.

D Reference to 'my invention being divided' suggests that he cannot decide which lie to tell next.

E 'with a grave nod' suggests Mr Pumblechook is taking the conversation very seriously.

F The sentences get longer to reflect the narrator's building worries.

Now read this exam-style question. **You don't need to answer it**. Instead think about what it is asking you to do, then answer the questions that follow.

Paper ①

3 In lines 46–53, how does the writer use language and structure to show that the narrator is getting into increasing difficulties? Support your views with reference to the text. **(6 marks)**

1 (a) Highlight which of the annotations A to F would help you to answer this exam-style question.

  (b) Circle or underline the annotation that relates to the structure of the extract.

  (c) Which detail above will **not** help you to answer the question? Explain your choice.

  The annotation that does not help answer the question is ....

  because ....

 Guided

2 Now read the whole extract from *Great Expectations* on page 96.

  Read the exam-style question below. **You do not need to answer it**. Instead, think about what it is asking you to do, then answer the question that follows.

Paper ①

4 In this extract, there is an attempt to show how the narrator is bullied by his aunt and Mr Pumblechook. Evaluate how successfully this is achieved. Support your views with detailed reference to the text. **(15 marks)**

 Guided

3 Choose four different-colour pens and assign one each to **setting**, **ideas**, **theme** or **events**. Annotate the extract from *Great Expectations* identifying words or phrases from these categories that would help you to answer the exam-style question above.

> When you are annotating, remember to identify setting, ideas, theme **and** events and make notes of the effect on the reader.

Putting it into practice

Read the full extract of *Middlemarch* on page 97, and the exam-style question below, then answer Questions 1 and 2.

Paper ①

3 In lines 20–30, how does the writer use language and structure to suggest that Fred is a source of disagreement between Mary and Rosamond?
Support your views with reference to the text.   **(6 marks)**

> **Guided** 1 (a) Highlight, circle or underline any words/phrases or structural devices in the extract that would help you to answer the exam-style question.

> **Remember**: structure is as important as language for this question.

(b) Make notes about the effect that four words/phrases or structural devices you have identified has on the reader.

....

....

....

....

....

> **Guided** 2 Now use your annotations and notes from Question 1 to write the first two paragraphs of an answer to the exam-style question.

> When you tackle this kind of question remember to:
> • spend about 12 minutes on your answer
> • highlight any key words in the question so you get the focus right
> • use only the lines of the text referred to in the question.

....

....

....

....

....

....

....

....

....

....

....

....

> **Remember**: You are only being asked to write part of an answer on this page. In the exam, you will be given more space to write a full answer.

Putting it into practice

Read the full extract of *Notes from a Small Island* on page 102, and the exam-style question below, then answer Questions 1 and 2.

Paper
②

6 Bill Bryson attempts to engage the reader with his entertaining description of his arrival at the hotel. Evaluate how successfully this is achieved.
Support your views with detailed reference to the text.   **(15 marks)**

 1 Highlight, circle or underline any words or phrases in the extract from *Notes from a Small Island* that would help you to answer the exam-style question.

 2 In one or two sentences, summarise your overall opinion on how successful Bill Bryson is in his attempt to entertain the reader.

....

....

....

....

> This question assesses **Assessment objective 4**: Evaluate texts critically and support this with appropriate textual references. This means you need to evaluate **ideas**, **events**, **themes** or **settings**. You are also required to make **critical judgements**.

 3 Now write the first two paragraphs of an answer to the exam-style question. Your summary from Question 2 can form the opening of your response and your annotations from Question 1 can be used as your evidence.

> When you tackle an AO4 question, remember to:
> • spend about 15 minutes on your answer
> • highlight any key words in the question so you get the focus right
> • focus on the way ideas and point of view are expressed by the writer
> • make judgements about the text and use language of critical judgement when making your points (for example, using adverbs such as 'effectively' and 'successfully' when commenting on how well the author has done something).

....

....

....

....

....

....

....

....

....

....

....

....

> **Remember**: You are only being asked to write part of an answer on this page. In the exam, you will be given more space to write a full answer.

Explicit information and ideas

Read the extract from *Middlemarch* below, then read the exam-style question.

There was a vague uneasiness associated with the word 'unsteady' which [Mary] hoped Rosamond might say something to dissipate³. But she purposely abstained⁴ from mentioning Mrs Waule's more special insinuation⁵.

'Oh, Fred is horrid!' said Rosamond. She would not have allowed herself so unsuitable a word to anyone but Mary.

'What do you mean by horrid?'

He is so idle, and makes Papa so angry, and says he will not take orders⁶.'

3: *dissipate* – make something disappear
4: *abstained* – stopped herself

5: *insinuation* – hint of something unpleasant
6: *orders* – a religious ceremony to become a clergyman

Paper ①

1 From lines 3–5, identify the phrase which explains why Mary is uncomfortable with how she has just described Fred. **(1 mark)**

1 Answer the exam-style question above.

....

> You don't need to closely read the whole extract if you are only being asked about two specific lines.

Now skim read the full extract from 'Wayward plastic' on page 104, then look at the exam-style question below. **You don't need to answer this question.** Instead, think about what it is asking you to do, then answer the questions that follow.

Paper ②

4 What was the cause of death of a young female sei whale in August 2014? **(1 mark)**

2 Circle the most effective way of answering the exam-style question above.

The cause of death was a broken DVD case

Broken DVD case

The cause of death for the young sei whale was a broken DVD case, which was found in her body

> For this 1 mark question, keep your answers as brief as possible – you don't need to waste time writing in full sentences.

3 Now skim read the full extract from 'Guidance from the Past' on page 103, then answer the exam-style questions below.

Paper ②

1 From lines 19–24, identify **two** qualities teenagers need to show. **(2 marks)**

(a) ....

(b) ....

Paper ②

4 In which year did Peter Scott post his tweet? **(1 mark)**

4 ....

Implicit ideas

Read this short extract from *Wuthering Heights*. Miss Dean is the housekeeper and the main narrator.

I sympathised awhile; but when the children fell ill of the measles, and I had to tend them, and take on me the cares of a woman at once, I changed my ideas. Heathcliff was dangerously sick; and while he lay at the worst he would have me constantly by his pillow: I suppose he felt I did a good deal for him, and he hadn't the wit to guess that I was compelled to do it. However, I will say this, he was the quietest child that ever a nurse watched over. The difference between him and the others forced me to be less partial. Cathy and her brother harassed me terribly; he was as uncomplaining as a lamb; though hardness, not gentleness, made him give little trouble.

Now look at this exam-style question relating to the text extract. **You don't need to answer it**. Instead answer Question 1 below.

Paper
①

2 From lines 8–11, give **two** reasons why Miss Dean prefers looking after Heathcliff. You may use your own words or quotations from the text.   **(2 marks)**

> To identify implicit ideas, you need to read between the lines and think about what the writer is suggesting or implying. Explicit ideas are not hidden – you just need to find short quotations or paraphrase what is already in the text.

1 Any two of these points could be used to answer the question. For each point, decide whether the information is explicit or implicit. The first one has been done for you.

(a) The children had the measles.   (Explicit)/Implicit

(b) The children were challenging to look after.   Explicit/Implicit

(c) The other two were very demanding, which meant looking after them was a more difficult task than looking after Heathcliff.   Explicit/Implicit

Now read this extract from *The Mayor of Casterbridge* before answering Question 2.

That laugh was not encouraging to strangers; and hence it may have been well that it was rarely heard. Many theories have been built upon it. It fell in well with conjectures[2] of a temperament which would have no pity for weakness, but it would be ready to yield ungrudging admiration to greatness and strength. Its producer's personal goodness, if he had any, would be of a very fitful cast – an occasional almost oppressive generosity rather than a mild and constant kindness.

2: *conjectures* – an opinion without all the information

2 Find three examples in the extract above that show the mayor is difficult to relate to. Your ideas may be explicit or implicit.

(a) ....

(b) ....

(c) ....

> Short answers on explicit and implicit information are usually only worth one mark for each point, so keep your answers brief. You can use your own words as well as quotations.

> In Paper 2, Questions 2 and 5 assess AO2. They are worth a low number of marks so you only need to comment on the language or structure, or give an example to support an idea.

Inference

Read this short extract from *Great Expectations*, then read the exam-style question below. **You do not need to answer it**. Instead think about what it is asking you to do. Then answer Questions 1 and 2 below.

unsuccessful

Mr Pumblechook and Mrs Joe stared at one another again in utter amazement. I was <u>perfectly frantic</u> – a reckless witness under the torture – and would have told them anything.
'Where *was* this coach, in the name of gracious?' asked my sister.
'In Miss Havisham's room.' They stared again. 'But there weren't any horses to it.' I added this saving clause, in the moment of rejecting four richly <u>caparisoned coursers</u> which I had wild thoughts of harnessing.

large powerful horses dressed in decorated cloth coverings —

Paper ①

4 In this extract, there is an attempt by the narrator to lie to Mrs Pumblechook and Mrs Joe about his encounter with Miss Havisham.
Evaluate how successfully this is achieved.
Support your views with detailed reference to the text.   **(15 marks)**

1 Highlight or underline any phrases in the extract that suggest successful or unsuccessful attempts by the narrator at lying. One is done for you.

2 What judgement can you make about the narrator in this extract? Use a short quotation to back up your answer.

> Being able to infer information from the text will help you answer Paper 1, Question 4 (AO4).

The extract suggests that the narrator ....

....

Quotation: ....

....

Now read this short extract, also from *Great Expectations*, and answer Question 3 below. In this extract, we read about the narrator's thoughts on his own behaviour as he tells his audience about his visit to Miss Havisham's.

'We played with flags,' I said. (I beg to observe that I think of myself with amazement, when I recall the lies I told on this occasion.)
'Flags!' echoed my sister.
'Yes,' said I. 'Estella waved a blue flag and I waved a red one, and Miss Havisham waved one sprinkled all over with little gold stars, out of the coach window. And then we all waved our swords and hurrahed.'
'Swords!' repeated my sister. 'Where did you get swords from?'
'Out of a cupboard,' said I. 'And I saw pistols in it – and jam – and pills. And there was no daylight in the room, but it was all lighted up with candles.'

3 Write about your impression of the narrator as suggested by what he tells us as readers and what he says to his audience.

The narrator is presented as someone who is not used to telling lies, shown by the words

....

> When thinking about the narrator in any fiction text you encounter, consider the thoughts shared with the reader and what the narrator's words and actions also suggest.

Interpreting information and ideas

Read this short extract from 'Freedom or death', then answer Question 1.

The grievances of those who have got power, the influence of those who have got power commands a great deal of attention; but the wrongs and the grievances of those people who have no power at all are apt to be absolutely ignored. That is the history of humanity right from the beginning. Well, in our civil war people have suffered, but you cannot make omelettes without breaking eggs; you cannot have civil war without damage to something. The great thing is to see that no more damage is done than is absolutely necessary, that you do just as much as will arouse enough feeling to bring about peace, to bring about an honourable peace for the combatants; and that is what we have been doing.

How words are used will affect their meaning according to their context. Look at the words and phrases that have been underlined in the extract above and how the words 'grievances' and 'commands' are used.

grievances: grudges, arguments: straightforward and expected use of this word

commands: *attracts, draws* (remember, this in the **context** of the text and this affects how the word is used): we expect it to be used in terms of orders/instructions, but here it is used to refer to attracting attention.

1 Now look at the three words below. Write what each word means within the **context** of the extract.

(a)   absolutely   ....

(b)   necessary   ....

(c)   combatants   ....

Try reading the text before and after the word or phrase you need to explain. This may help you to infer meaning. Remember that words and phrases can mean different things depending on the topic of the whole text.

Now read this short extract also from *Wuthering Heights*, then answer Question 2.

He was not insolent to his benefactor, he was simply insensible; though knowing perfectly the hold he had on his heart, and conscious he had only to speak and all the house obliged to bend to his wishes.

2 Underline words used in this extract which create an impression of Heathcliff's influence in the house. Two have been done for you. Then choose **two** of the words and explain their effect.

(a)   ....

....

(b)   ....

....

Using evidence

Read this short extract from 'Wayward plastic' then answer Question 1.

> The whale skeleton is a <u>profound</u> statement about the unintended consequences and <u>unexpected costs</u> of our way of life. It's a statement that needs a meaningful response, but it would be <u>hypocritical</u> of me to say we should stop using plastic altogether. I know I don't want to live in a world without whales, but I'm not sure that I want to live in a world without plastic either.

> Use single word quotations from the text carefully. When you are embedding them as part of a sentence, the sentence should make sense when you read it back.

1   In your answers to both the fiction text in Paper 1 (Questions 3 and 4) and the non-fiction text in Paper 2 (Questions 2, 3 and 6), you will be asked to support your views with references to the text. Two short quotations are underlined in the extract above to support your explanation of the writer's views about the situation with whales. The first part of the explanation has been done for you. Try to finish the answer.

The writer is very affected by the skeleton of the whale because the whale had been killed

by eating plastics. This makes the death 'profound' because of what it is telling us about

how plastic is killing marine wildlife. The writer realises that as human beings this is not what

we wanted to happen – this is 'unintended'. She uses the phrase 'unexpected costs' which

suggests that ....

....

....

....

> In the exam you may want to underline evidence in the extract that you will use to support your answers.

Read this short extract, also from 'Wayward plastic', then answer Question 2.

> I can't change what was, but I can help change what will be. The reusable shopping bag is such a little thing, but it matters. And every one of us who bring our own bags can know – from this day forward – that none of the plastic shopping bags that find their way to the ocean ever belonged to us.

> Paraphrasing can be useful way to support your points when you are evaluating a text as a whole. However, remember to use your own words along with short quotations when analysing language.

2   When you paraphrase, you use your own words. When you are quoting directly from the text, you place words and phrases in quotation marks. Complete the following explanation by paraphrasing the information in the extract above.

The writer knows that we cannot alter what has happened in the past but she feels that we

can ....

> When using quotations, remember that:
> • short quotations are most effective
> • you must use quotations rather than paraphrasing when explaining the effects of language
> • all quotations must be in quotation marks and copied correctly from the text
> • long quotations can make it unclear which part is supporting the point made.

Point – Evidence – Explain

Read this short extract from 'Guidance from the Past' and the exam-style question below. **You do not need to answer it**. Then answer the questions below.

> 'You're supposed to be mature enough to accept some of the responsibility your parents have carried for years. They have nursed, protected, helped, appealed, begged, excused, tolerated and denied themselves needed comforts so that you could have every benefit. This they have done gladly, for you are their dearest treasure. But now, you have no right to expect them to bow to every whim and fancy just because selfish ego, instead of common sense, dominates your personality, thinking and requests.
>
> 'In heaven's name, grow up and go home!'

Paper ②

3 Analyse how the writer uses language and structure to interest and engage readers. Support your views with detailed reference to the text.   **(15 marks)**

1 Fill in the blanks in this student's P–E–E response to the exam-style question.

Make your point: The writer uses several verbs to show ....
Provide evidence to support your point: For example, 'nursed', '.................................. ....
Introduce your explanation: This gives the impression that ....

> **Remember:** Think about not only the point – using verbs – and the evidence, but also the effect of this technique in presenting an idea. Think about how this engages the reader.

2 Reread the extract and then look at the point below. Select evidence from the extract to support this point.

Point: The writer uses several adjectives to describe the contrast between how parents regard teenagers, and how teenagers behave.

For example, she uses the words ....
....

> Point–Evidence–Explain is useful if you are asked to comment on language and structure, or to evaluate or compare a text. Improve your P–E–E paragraphs by using more than one piece of evidence to support your point. In some cases, you may use PETER: Point–Evidence–Technique–Explain–Reader's response.

Putting it into practice

Guided 1 Read the full extract from *Middlemarch* on page 97, then answer the exam-style questions below.

Paper ① 1 From lines 1–4, identify the phrase which suggests that Fred thinks a lot of himself.   **(1 mark)**

(a) ....

Paper ① 2 From lines 7–10, give **two** ways that Rosamond shows she takes herself very seriously.   **(2 marks)**

(b) ....

....

....

Guided 2 Now write a P–E–E paragraph to answer the exam-style question below.

> When you tackle this kind of question in the exam, remember to:
> • spend about 12 minutes on your answer
> • identify the main focus of the question
> • read the text carefully and annotate it with your ideas
> • only use the lines of the extract referred to in the question.

Paper ① 3 In lines 12–30, how does the writer use language and structure to create the disagreement between Mary and Rosamond?
Support your views with reference to the text.   **(6 marks)**

....

....

....

....

....

....

....

....

....

....

....

....

> **Remember:** You are only being asked to write part of an answer on this page. In the exam, you will be given more space to write a full answer.

Putting it into practice

> The exam-style question below is for Paper 2 and assesses AO2. It carries 15 marks so make sure you spend enough time to develop your ideas fully. For questions carrying more marks, it is important that you keep to the point and answer the question throughout.

1 Read the full extract from 'Wayward plastic' on page 104. Then write three P–E–E paragraphs of an answer to the exam-style question below.

> When you tackle this kind of question in the exam, remember to:
> - spend about 15 minutes on your answer
> - read the question carefully and highlight the main focus
> - read the text carefully and annotate it with your ideas
> - refer to the whole text as no line numbers are given in the question
> - comment on how the writer uses language and structure and what the effects are on the reader.

Paper ②

3 Analyse how the writer uses language and structure to interest and engage readers. Support your view with detailed references to the text. **(15 marks)**

....
....
....
....
....
....
....
....
....
....
....
....
....
....
....
....
....
....
....

> **Remember**: You are only being asked to write part of an answer on this page. In the exam, you will be given more space to write a full answer.

> Although Question 3 in Paper 1 also assesses AO2, it is only for 6 marks. That means you must make every word count.

Word classes

Read the short extract from 'Wayward plastic', then answer Questions 1 and 2.

> There might be ways to compromise. More attention is being put <u>towards</u> manufacturing biodegradable plastics. Plastic bans or taxes are being implemented around the world. As of May 2014, there were 77 countries with plastic bag reduction policies and 133 cities in the United States with anti-plastic bag legislation according to an Earth Policy Institute analysis. And the policies help. The Portland Bureau of Planning and Sustainability found that in just one year after a plastic bag ban was put in place, the use of <u>reusable</u> bags increased by 304%.

1 Circle and label at least one example of each of the following word classes: noun, adjective, verb and preposition. Two have been done for you.

> • **noun** – is the name of a thing, place or idea (pen, builder, hospital or happiness)
> • **verb** – usually describes an action, either physical or mental (shouting, ran, believe, considering)
> • **adverb** – gives more information about the verb ('The boy ran <u>quickly</u>')
> • **adjective** – describes a noun ('The <u>large</u> dog splashed in the <u>filthy</u> puddle'). Adjectives can be compound (joined with a hyphen, such as 'multi-million').
> Adjectives can become comparatives (e.g. noisier, more insolent) and superlatives (noisiest, most insolent).

Below is a question designed to get you thinking about how verbs are used.

> If you do not remember the different verb forms, you can still write about their effects. For example, you could write: 'The writer uses the verb "might" which suggests …'

2 The writer uses the modal verb 'might'. What effect does this have on the reader?

The modal verb 'might' suggests ....

....

....

3 Now read lines 13–18 from *The Mayor of Casterbridge* on page 98.
In this extract, the writer uses adjectives and verbs to describe the encounter with the mayor. What effect do these have on the reader?

Adjectives			Verbs
keen	broad (chest)	encumbered	regarded / looked at / assessed
The adjective 'keen' suggests that Elizabeth is very interested in the mayor and what she is witnessing	....	....	....

Connotations

Read this short extract from *Notes from a Small Island*, then answer Question 1.

> Among the many <u>gleaming palaces of comfort</u> that lined every street for blocks around, I selected an establishment on a side-street for no good reason other than that I rather liked its sign: neat capitals in pink neon <u>glowing beckoningly</u> through the slicing rain. I stepped inside, shedding water and could see at a glance it was a good choice – clean, nicely old-fashioned, <u>attractively priced at £26 B&B</u> according to a notice on the wall, and with the kind of <u>smothering warmth</u> that makes your glasses steam and brings on sneezing fits. I <u>decanted</u> several ounces of water from my sleeve and asked for a single room for two nights.

> When we read a text, there are different layers of meaning. For example, 'it was a good choice' in the extract above has a literal meaning as there is no hidden connotation. In contrast, although here 'gleaming palaces of comfort' means 'luxurious-looking hotels', the idea of something luxurious/palatial is further connoted from the original phrase referring to the 'gleaming palaces' (or 'shining castles').

1 (a) Look at the phrases underlined, taken from the above text. Complete the table by writing the connotations suggested by the underlined words. One has been done for you.

gleaming palaces of comfort	luxurious-looking hotels
glowing beckoningly	
smothering warmth	so hot it is overwhelming
decanted	
attractively priced at £26 B&B	

(b) Use your answers above to answer the following question:

What impressions of the writer's situation do the underlined words and phrases suggest to the reader?

The phrase 'gleaming palaces of comfort' suggests places which are height of luxury and

comfort. The adjective 'gleaming' suggests ....

....

....

....

Now read this short extract from *Wuthering Heights*, then answer Question 2.

> ... still I couldn't <u>dote</u> on Heathcliff, and I wondered often what my master saw to admire so much in the sullen boy who never, to my recollection, repaid his indulgence by any sign of gratitude. He was not <u>insolent</u> to his <u>benefactor</u>, he was simply insensible ...

└fuss about and be fond of

└disrespectful

someone who gives money ──┘

2 Circle two words from the extract above which suggest that Heathcliff and his benefactor view their relationship differently.

Explain how the two words you circled convey that meaning.

(a) ....

....

(b) ....

....

Figurative language

Read this short extract from *Great Expectations*, then answer Question 1.

> 'Immense,' said I. 'And they fought for <u>veal</u> cutlets out of a silver casket.'
> Mr Pumblechook and Mrs Joe stared at one another again in utter amazement. I was perfectly
> frantic – a reckless witness under the torture – and would have told them anything.

└─thin slices of calf meat

1 What does the metaphor 'a reckless witness under the torture' suggest about how the narrator feels?

The metaphor 'a reckless witness under the torture' suggests that the narrator feels ....

....

This suggests to the reader ....

....

....

Now read this short extract from *Wuthering Heights*, then answer Question 2.

> Cathy and her brother harassed me terribly: he was as uncomplaining as a lamb; though hardness,
> not gentleness, made him give little trouble.

Guided

2 (a) Identify one simile from the extract above.

....

> You could identify the simile by underlining it, which is good practice for looking at texts
> in detail and picking out examples/references to help you answer questions in the exam.

(b) Write one or two sentences commenting on why the writer has used your identified simile and
its effect on the reader. You could write about how it engages the reader/helps to create an
impression or image.

....

....

Now read this short extract from *The Mayor of Casterbridge*, then answer Question 3.

> Time, the magician, had wrought much here. Watching him, and thus thinking of past days, she
> became so moved that she shrank back against the jamb[6] of the waggon-office doorway to which
> the steps gave access, the shadow from it conveniently hiding her features.

6: *jamb* – post or side of a doorway

Guided

3 (a) Identify where the writer has used personification by annotating on the extract above.

(b) Write one or two sentences commenting on the way the writer has used your identified
personification and its effect on the reader.

....

....

....

> **Remember**: It is not enough to just identify and name a figurative device used in the
> text. You need to comment on **why** the writer has used it and its **effect** on the reader.

Creation of character

Read the short extract from *Wuthering Heights*, then answer Question 1.

> Heathcliff took the handsomest, but it soon fell lame, and when he discovered it, he said to Hindley, 'You must exchange horses with me; I don't like mine, and if you won't I shall tell your father of the three lashings you've given me this week, and show him my arm, which is black to the shoulder.' Hindley put out his tongue and cuffed him over the ears.
> 'You'd better do it at once,' he persisted, escaping to the porch (they were in the stable): 'you will have to; and if I speak of these blows, you'll get them again with interest.'
> 'Off dog!' cried Hindley, threatening him with an iron weight, used for weighing potatoes and hay.
> 'Throw it,' he replied, standing still, 'and then I'll tell how you boasted that you would turn me out of doors as soon as he died, and see whether he will not turn you out directly.'
> Hindley threw it, hitting him on the breast, and down he fell, but staggered up immediately, breathless and white...

1 Complete the table to show how the writer uses dialogue, action and description to build up ideas about the characters.

> You can get an impression of a character from:
> * what they **do** (actions)
> * what they **say** or what is said about them (dialogue)
> * how they are **described** (descriptions)

Use of dialogue	Use of action	Use of description
Heathcliff's words, ...	Heathcliff's actions, ...	....
....	....	....
....	....	....
....	....	....
....	....	....
....	....	....

Now reread the extract from *Wuthering Heights*, then answer Question 2.

2 How do Heathcliff's words and actions in the extract above build up an idea of both his character and the character of Hindley?

....

....

....

Turn to the full extract of *Wuthering Heights* on page 99. Read the final paragraph.

3 Write a Point–Evidence–Explanation paragraph showing how the writer creates more ideas about Hindley. Use the prompts below to help you.

Point: Hindley is ....

Evidence: This is shown by ....

Explanation: This suggests that ....

....

> This is just an example of how you can structure a response. With practice, you will be able to make the point and provide the evidence and explanation in ways that better suit you.

Creating atmosphere

Read this short extract from *The Mayor of Casterbridge*, then answer Question 1.

> <u>Time, the magician</u>, had wrought much here. Watching him, and thus thinking of past days, she became so moved that she shrank back against the jamb[6] of the waggon-office doorway to which the steps gave access, the shadow from it conveniently hiding her features. She forgot her daughter till a touch from Elizabeth-Jane aroused her. 'Have you seen him, mother?' whispered the girl. 'Yes, yes,' answered her companion hastily. 'I have seen him, and it is enough for me! Now I want to go – pass away – die.'

6: *jamb* – post or side of a doorway

1 Underline **three** examples of language that creates atmosphere in the extract. Write a sentence for each one that describes the overall mood or tone that is created.

The personification of time as 'the magician' creates a mood of ....

....

....

....

....

Now read this short extract, also from *The Mayor of Casterbridge*. Then answer Questions 2 and 3.

> He was dressed in an old-fashioned evening suit, an expanse of frilled shirt showing on his broad breast, jewelled studs, and a heavy gold chain. Three glasses stood at his right hand; but, to his wife's surprise, the two for wine were empty, while the third, a tumbler, was half full of water. When last she had seen him he was sitting in a corduroy[3] jacket, fustian[4] waistcoat and breeches, and tanned leather leggings, with a basin of hot furmity[5] before him.

3: *corduroy* – a fabric made up of a cord pattern
4: *fustian* – heavily woven, coarse cotton cloth
5: *furmity* – dish of wheat boiled in milk with cinnamon

2 In the extract above, the writer contrasts the mayor as he was years ago with how he is now. Identify the words and phrases which create this contrast and write two or three sentences explaining how they contribute to the change in atmosphere in the extract.

In the extract, the mayor is wearing an 'evening suit'. The adjectives used by the writer create an

atmosphere of ....

....

....

> When you answer a question about language techniques in the exam, start with an overview to summarise the overall effect of the extract.

3 Look again at your answer to Question 2. Use the ideas there to write a sentence relating to the overall atmosphere created in the extract above.

Overall, the writer creates an atmosphere of ....

....

....

Narrative voice

Read extracts 1, 2 and 3 below.

Extract 1: from *Middlemarch*

'I wish no one said any worse of him. He should be more careful. Mrs Waule has been telling uncle that Fred is very unsteady.' Mary spoke from a girlish impulse which got the better of her judgement. There was a vague uneasiness associated with the word 'unsteady' which she hoped Rosamond might say something to dissipate³. But she purposely abstained⁴ from mentioning Mrs Waule's more special insinuation⁵.

3: *dissipate* – make something disappear   5: *insinuation* – hint of something unpleasant
4: *abstained* – stopped herself

Extract 2: from *Great Expectations*

If they had asked me any more questions I should undoubtedly have betrayed myself, for I was even then on the point of mentioning that there was a balloon in the yard, and should have hazarded⁸ the statement but for my invention being divided between that phenomenon and a bear in the brewery⁹. They were so much occupied, however, in discussing the marvels I had already presented for their consideration, that I escaped.

8: *hazarded* – guessed without confidence   9: *brewery* – a place where beer is made

Extract 3: from *Wuthering Heights*

Hindley threw it, hitting him on the breast, and down he fell, but staggered up immediately, breathless and white; and, had I not prevented it, he would have gone just so to the master, and got full revenge by letting his condition plead for him, intimating who had caused it.

Now read the descriptions of the narrative voices below, then answer Questions 1 and 2.

A

First-person narrative has been used to show the reader how serious the situation became and the role of the narrator in stopping things from becoming much worse.

B

Third person narrative has been used. This 'omniscient narrator' knows everything and is able to tell us about the characters' thoughts, words and actions.

C   Great Expectations

First-person narrative has been used to tell the reader just how far the narrator was prepared to go if more was required in terms of information.

1 Match each extract to the description of the narrative voice. One has been done for you.

> Narrative voice is the 'voice' a writer of fiction chooses to tell the story. A writer can choose a narrative voice to create a particular point of view.

2 Reread Extract 2. How does the first-person narrative voice involve the reader in the narrator's recounting of his visit to Miss Havisham?

The first person narrative involves the reader by ....

....

....

....

Putting it into practice

1 Read the full extract from *Wuthering Heights* on page 99, then answer the exam-style question below.

Paper ①

3 In lines 22–32, how does the writer use language and structure to present the violent relationship between Heathcliff and Hindley?
Support your views with reference to the text.

(6 mark)

> When you tackle this type of question in the exam, remember to:
> • spend about 12 minutes on your answer
> • read the question carefully and highlight the main focus
> • read the source text thoroughly, annotating as you read
> • only use the lines of the text referred to in the question
> • identify the language and structure devices and comment on their effects
> • support all your points with clear evidence and a clear explanation by using the P–E–E structure in your paragraphs.

> In the exam you will need to write about language and structure to answer this kind of question. Focus on how the writer uses language – skills you have already covered in detail in this Workbook – but make some comments on structure too. You can refer back and add to these when you have looked at structure further.

....
....
....
....
....
....
....
....
....
....
....
....
....
....
....
....
....
....

> **Remember**: You are only being asked to write part of an answer on this page. In the exam, you will be given more space to write a full answer.

Rhetorical devices 1

Read this short extract from 'Wayward plastic', then answer Questions 1 and 2.

> My first thought is that I have two antsy kids with me who have their hearts set on eating today –
> but a second later, I find myself thinking about that dead sperm whale I saw on Warderick Wells Cay
> in The Bahamas.
> The connection between the two? The plastic bags.
>
> **Plastics: 1, Marine Mammals: 0**
> Plastic bags, plastic cups, plastic sheeting, plastic bottles, plastic toys, plastic, plastic, plastic.
> There's even a patch of Pacific Ocean – thought to be at least the size of Texas and dubbed the
> Great Pacific Garbage Patch – comprised of plastic and other trash, bobbing along at the surface,
> circling in the current.

1 Find four of the following rhetorical devices in the extract above. Circle them below and label
   them in the extract. One has been done for you.
   • pattern of three
   • lists
   • alliteration
   • colloquial language
   • question followed by answer (hypophora)

2 For each device you have identified, write one or more sentences commenting on:
   • why the writer has used it
   • the intended effect on the reader.

The answer has been started for you, with comments about the writer's use of lists.

> Remember to think about how rhetorical devices are used by considering their effect on the reader.

The writer uses a list to emphasise how much plastic we use in the world: 'plastic bags, plastic

cups, plastic sheeting'. As it is part of her wider article about plastic, it makes the reader aware

that this is a big problem. The writer also ....

....

....

....

....

....

....

....

....

....

....

....

....

Rhetorical devices 2

Read this short extract from 'Freedom or death', then answer Questions 1 and 2.

It is about eight years since the word <u>militant</u> was first used to describe what we were doing. It was not militant at all, except that it provoked militancy on the part of those who were opposed to it. When women asked questions in political meetings and failed to get answers, they were not doing anything militant. In Great Britain it is a custom, a time-honoured one, to ask questions of candidates for parliament and ask questions of members of the government. No man was ever put out of a public meeting for asking a question. The first people who were put out of a political meeting for asking questions were women; they were brutally ill-used; they found themselves in jail before 24 hours had expired.

└─someone using conflict or violence to achieve a cause

1 Annotate the extract to show any language or rhetorical devices that the writer has used to emphasise their points. The following devices might help you.

repetition   **emotive language**   **contrast**

Guided **2** The writer is very aware of how women are presented in their fight for the right to vote. How does the repetition of 'militant' and 'questions' help to present her viewpoint?

'militant': ....

....

'questions': ....

....

Now read this short extract, also from 'Freedom or death', then answer Question 3.

You have two babies very hungry and wanting to be fed. <u>One baby is a patient baby, and waits indefinitely</u> until its mother is ready to feed it. The <u>other baby is an impatient baby and cries lustily, screams and kicks</u> and makes everybody unpleasant until it is fed. Well, we know perfectly well which baby is attended to first.

Look at how the writer describes different babies to make her point about the impact of different types of behaviour.

3 Write one or two sentences explaining how the writer contrasts the different babies to present her argument about the need for action instead of waiting for change.

The writer refers to two babies who are both very hungry but behave differently. One is very loud

and the other is very patient. She then goes on to explain ....

....

....

Read the rest of the extract on page 100, then answer Question 4.

> If you know it, use the technical name for a device in your answer. If you don't know the name, you should still comment on the language and effect, referring to it as the 'device' when commenting.

4 Identify one example of a list of actions and one example of a metaphor in the extract. Then write a sentence for each on why the writer has used this rhetorical device and its effect on the reader.

pattern of three ....

metaphor ....

Fact, opinion and expert evidence

1 Draw lines to link the words in bold with the correct definition and example.

Something known to be true	**Fact**	Ed Sheeran is superior to all other musicians
The opinion of a person or group with special knowledge about a subject	**Opinion**	Malala Yousafzai was born on 12 July 1997
Something a person believes that may or may not be true	**Expert evidence**	You should improve your diet and do more exercise to give you the best chance of living longer

Now read the following three quotations from 'Are fidget spinners a scam?', then answer Question 2.

A Dr Rapport's 2015 study found that children with ADHD who participated in activities involving 'gross body movement' … performed better than those who sat still during memory tasks.
B [Fidget spinners] vary in cost between $1 for standard spinners, to $59.99 …
C The device has made her daughter less stressed and self-conscious about her need to fidget at school.

2 Identify which of the above quotations (A, B or C) is being presented as a fact, an opinion or expert advice. One has been done for you.

(a) a fact ...B....   (b) an opinion ....   (c) expert evidence ....

> Think about how the use of fact, opinion and expert evidence helps to support the writer's viewpoint or argument. This will be useful preparation for Paper 2.

Now read another short extract from 'Are fidget spinners a scam?' below. Then answer Question 3.

The devices are also regularly marketed for helping to provide increased focus and stress relief for people who have Attention Deficit Disorder (ADD), Attention Deficit Hyperactivity Disorder (ADHD), Anxiety and Autism – however, there is no proof to support this claim. Dr Mark Rapport, MD and Director of the Children's Learning Clinic at the University of Central Florida's Department of Psychology, told the DailyMail.com that while his current and past research indicates that many children with ADHD benefit from some forms of movement when engaged in challenging cognitive tasks, he has not come across any studies examining the potential benefits or adverse effects of fidget spinners.

3 (a) Look again at the extract and identify one fact, one opinion and one piece of expert evidence used to support the writer's viewpoint. Highlight or underline these in the extract above.

   (b) Write a sentence for each example you have identified in Question 3 (a), and explain how the writer uses this to support their viewpoint.

Fact ....

Opinion ....

....

Expert evidence ....

....

> **Remember**: The person providing the expert evidence can also be the author of the text.

27

Identifying sentence types

> You are asked to comment on language and structure in both Paper 1 (responding to fiction) and Paper 2 (responding to non-fiction). You will write about paragraphing and layout where appropriate, but also how the writer uses sentence structure.

1 Look carefully at the four sentences below. Each one is a different type of sentence, but which is which? Draw lines to match the sentences (a) to (d) to the correct sentence type.

(a) I was very happy.

(b) The streets were full of swishing cars, their headlights sweeping through bullets of shiny rain.

(c) Night had fallen heavily and the streets were full of swishing cars.

(d) Complete meltdown.

> minor sentence
>
> multi-clause sentence (coordinate)
>
> multi-clause sentence (subordinate)
>
> single-clause sentence

Now read this short extract from *Notes from a Small Island*, then answer Question 2.

> By the time I reached the East Cliff, a neighbourhood of medium-sized hotels perched high above a black sea, I was soaked through and muttering. The only thing to be said for Bournemouth is that you are certainly spoiled for choice with hotels. Among the many gleaming palaces of comfort that lined every street for blocks around, I selected an establishment on a side-street for no good reason other than that I rather liked its sign: neat capitals in pink neon glowing beckoningly through the slicing rain. I stepped inside, shedding water and could see at a glance it was a good choice – clean, nicely old-fashioned, attractively priced at £26 B&B according to a notice on the wall, and with the kind of smothering warmth that makes your glasses steam and brings on sneezing fits. I decanted several ounces of water from my sleeve and asked for a single room for two nights.

2 In the extract above, highlight or circle one example of the following sentence types: **single clause**, **multi-clause** (subordinate) and **multi-clause** (coordinate).

> • Single-clause sentences are made up of just **one clause** and provide **one piece of information** about an event or action. They contain **a subject** and **one verb**.
> • Multi-clause sentences are made up of **more than one clause**. They contain **two or more verbs**.
> • Subordinate clauses do not make sense on their own. They are **dependent** on the main clause.
> • Co-ordinate clauses are an **equal pair**, where neither clause is dependent on the other.
> • Minor sentences are grammatically incomplete because they **do not contain a verb**.
> There are some exceptions; for example, 'I arrived at five thirty in the evening in a driving rain' has two pieces of information, but only one verb ('driving' is used as an adjective).

3 Choose one of the sentence types you identified in Question 2. Write some notes about the effect of using this sentence type in the text.

....

....

....

....

....

> **Remember:** In the exam you will need to comment on the effect of the sentence choices; it is not enough to simply identify them.

Commenting on sentence types

Read this short extract from *I am Malala*, then answer Question 1.

> It will never be Swat, which I miss every day, but these days, when I travel to other places and return to this new house, it does feel like home. I have even stopped thinking about the constant rain, although I laugh when my friends here complain about the heat when it's 68 or 77 degrees Fahrenheit. To me that feels like spring. I am making friends at my new school, although Moniba is still my best friend and we Skype for hours at a time to catch up on everything. When she talks about parties back in Swat, I so wish I was there.

1   The writer of the extract above uses a variety of sentence types. How do these sentence structures reflect the narrator's feelings? Use the following words to help you.

multi-clause sentences (subordinate)   short sentences   reminiscing   factual

The narrator uses .... to describe ....

....

....

....

Now read this short extract from *The Mayor of Casterbridge* in which Elizabeth talks to her mother about the mayor.

> 'Why – Oh what?' She drew closer, and whispered in her mother's ear, 'Does he seem to you not likely to befriend us? I thought he looked a generous man. What a gentleman he is, isn't he? And how his diamond studs shine! How strange that you should have said he might be in the stocks, or in the workhouse, or dead!'

2   In this extract the writer uses a variety of sentence lengths to show the difference between how Elizabeth's mother described the mayor's possible situation and his current position in Casterbridge. Explain how the sentence structure is used to present Elizabeth's reaction.

The writer starts the paragraph with a short question to show that Elizabeth is feeling ....

.... This is immediately followed by a multi-clause sentence to describe

her interaction with her mother as Elizabeth wants to know answers. She follows this with ......

....

The writer uses a single-clause sentence to build up Elizabeth's excitement: 'And how his diamond

studs shine!' This is followed by ....

....

Turn to the full extract on page 98 and read the closing two lines, then answer Question 3.

3   Write one or two sentences explaining how the sentence structure continues to show Elizabeth's excitement.

> It is very important to comment on how the writer used structure together with the language in order to create an effect.

....

....

Structure: non-fiction

Read the opening and closing sentences of 'Guidance from the Past'. Then answer Questions 1 and 2.

> I'm sure you've heard that common complaint of teenagers all over the world: 'That's boring', 'This is boring' or simply 'I'm bored'.
>
> …
>
> *'Be bored or don't be: just stop complaining about it!'*

1   Complete the table. Write down the effect of using this structural technique in the opening sentence.

Structural technique	Effect
• Direct address used in the opening sentence	....

> Punctuation also counts as a structural feature and you can analyse punctuation for AO2.

2   Consider the following ways in which writers can end their writing in order to leave a lasting impression.

> warnings or consequences   calls to action   positivity/upbeat   summary of main points

(a)   Circle the device you think best describes the way the article ends in 'Guidance from the Past'.

(b)   Explain why you think the writer chose to end in that way. Remember to comment on **effect**.

....

Read these short extracts from 'Wayward plastic'. The second one is from later in the article. Then answer Question 3 below.

> That same year, scientists reviewed seabird necropsies (an autopsy of an animal) and found that 90% of seabirds found dead on the beach have ingested plastic.
>
> …
>
> Certainly, this isn't a silver bullet to solve our plastic addiction, but it is an important move toward a world where my convenience doesn't come at the direct cost of another creature's health.

3   Non-fiction writers need to keep the interest of their readers and also be persuasive. They often do this by changing the tone or focus of their writing to present their argument in different ways. How does Byington do this in the extracts from 'Wayward plastic' above?

Byington uses statistics to support her argument that the use of plastics is destroying wildlife.

She refers to 90% of seabirds who have 'ingested' plastic and it is implied that this is linked to

the cause of death. She later starts to write about possible solutions when she ....

....

....

Structure: fiction

Read the extract from *Wuthering Heights*. Now focus on these lines from the extract and then answer Question 1.

> ... the young master had learnt to regard his father as an oppressor rather than a friend, and Heathcliff as a usurper of his father's affections, and his privileges, and <u>he grew bitter with brooding over these injuries.</u>

1 There is conflict that occurs between Hindley and Heathcliff later in novel. How does the phrase underlined in the short extract above foreshadow this conflict?

> Remember that foreshadowing is an advanced sign or warning of what is to come in the future.

The words 'bitter brooding' suggest that Hindley ....

....

....

....

Now read this short extract from *Great Expectations*, then answer Question 2.

> 'Boy! What like is Miss Havisham?' Mr Pumblechook began again when he had recovered; folding his arms tight on his chest and applying the screw.
> 'Very tall and dark,' I told him.
> 'Is she, uncle?' asked my sister.
> Mr Pumblechook winked assent; from which I inferred that he had never seen Miss Havisham, for she was nothing of the kind.

2 Here the writer describes the beginning of the interview about the visit to Miss Havisham's. Write one or two sentences explaining the effect of the writer's choice of sentence types and dialogue on the reader. You can use the following words to help you.

| figurative language | dialogue | beginning with a question |

....

....

....

....

....

Read the full extract from *Great Expectations* on page 96, focusing on the final paragraph. Now reread the short extract that you explored in Question 2. Then answer Question 3.

3 Write one or two sentences to show how the descriptions of the characters' words and actions in the short extract above serve as a build up to the final paragraph in the full extract. You may use your answer to Question 2 as the starting point.

> **Remember:** Writers of fiction use a variety of narrative structures for effect. These include foreshadowing, use of detail or action, repetition and dialogue. This means you need to write about language **and** structure.

....

....

....

....

....

31

Putting it into practice

  1 Read the full extract of *Middlemarch* on page 97, then answer the exam-style question below.

 Paper ①

> **3** In lines 31–37, how does the writer use language and structure to present the characters of Mary and Rosamond?
>
> **(6 marks)**

> When you tackle this type of question in the exam, remember to:
> • spend about 12 minutes on your answer
> • read the question carefully and highlight the main focus
> • read the source text thoroughly, annotating as you read
> • only use the lines of the text referred to in the question
> • identify the language and structure devices and comment on their effects
> • support all your points with clear evidence and a clear explanation by using the P–E–E structure in your paragraphs.

> In the exam you will need to write about language **and** structure to answer this kind of question. You mainly practised language on page 24. Here write about both language **and** structure.

....

....

....

....

....

....

....

....

....

....

....

....

....

....

....

....

....

....

....

....

Putting it into practice

Guided 1 Read the full extract from *I am Malala* on page 105, then answer the exam-style question below.

Paper
②   3 Analyse how the writer uses language and structure to interest and engage readers. Support your views with detailed reference to the text.   **(15 marks)**

> When you tackle this type of question in the exam, remember to:
> • spend about 15 minutes on your answer
> • read the question carefully and annotate it with your ideas
> • refer to the whole text as no line numbers are given
> • identify the language and structural techniques and comment on their effects
> • support all your points with clear evidence and a clear explanation by using the P–E–E structure in your paragraphs.

> **Remember**: Although Paper 1, Question 3 asks you to analyse language and structure, it is only for 6 marks. This Paper 2 question is for 15 marks, so will require more detail in your answer. For both answers, you will need to comment on language **and** structure.

....
....
....
....
....
....
....
....
....
....
....
....
....
....
....
....
....
....
....

> **Remember:** You have more space than this to answer your question in the exam. Use your own paper to finish your answer to the question above.

Handling two texts

In Paper 2, your ability to handle two texts together will be tested. Question 7 (a) will test AO1(b) and Question 7 (b) will assess AO3.

Read the assessment objectives below, then answer Questions 1 and 2.

Assessment objective 1(b)
Select and synthesise evidence from different texts

Assessment objective 3
Compare writer's ideas and perspectives, as well as how these are conveyed, across two or more texts

'Synthesise' means to bring things together. These synonyms also mean synthesise: combine, fuse, amalgamate, blend and mix.

1 Which of the assessment objectives above will require you to identify **and** explain both similarities **and** differences between the texts?

....

Now look at these exam-style questions. **You don't need to answer these questions**. Instead, think about how they test the skills in AO1(b) and AO3, then answer Question 3.

Paper ②

7 (a) The two texts are both about family relationships.
What are the similarities between the family relationships?
Use evidence from both texts to support your answer.   **(6 marks)**

(b) Compare how the writers of 'Guidance from the Past' and *I am Malala* present their ideas and perspectives about family life.
Support your answer with detailed references to the texts.   **(14 marks)**

2 Read the statements below. Decide which paper or question each statement describes. Circle your choices.

(a) The two non-fiction texts will always be linked by a common theme or topic, so they will always have something in common.   **Paper 1   Paper 2**

(b) This question will test Assessment objective 3 by asking you to compare the texts.
                                                                     Question 7 (a)   Question 7 (b)

(c) This question will test Assessment objective 1(b) by asking you to synthesise information from both texts.   **Question 7 (a)   Question 7 (b)**

(d) This question is only worth 6 marks so you should make about three or four points.
                                                                     Question 7 (a)   Question 7 (b)

(e) This question is worth 14 marks, so you should spend more time on this question.
                                                                     Question 7 (a)   Question 7 (b)

(f) For this question, you will need to compare language and structure as well as looking at the writers' attitudes and ideas.   **Question 7 (a)   Question 7 (b)**

(g) For this question, you should start by giving an overview to show your understanding of the question.   **Question 7 (a)   Question 7 (b)**

Selecting evidence for synthesis

Read the full texts of 'Freedom or death' on page 100 and 'Wayward plastic' on page 104. Then read the exam-style question below. **You don't need to answer this question.** Instead, think about what it is asking you to do, then answer Questions 1 and 2.

Paper ②

7 **(a)**   The two texts are about taking action.
   What similarities are there between the ways to take action?
   Use evidence from the text to support your answer.   **(6 marks)**

> Skim read the first text to find your evidence then select evidence from the second text to combine with it.

> Only 6 marks are available for this question, so think about the amount of reading time and the time you should spend answering this question.

1   The above question identifies a similar idea shared by both texts: the need to take action. Complete the table below.

Taking action: similarity	
Extract 1	**Extract 2**
Emmeline Pankhurst says that 'you have to make more noise than anybody else'	Byington says that ....

 2   Write down one more piece of evidence from each text that supports the similar idea shared by both texts: the need to take action.

'Freedom or death': ....
....
'Wayward plastic': ....
....

Read the exam-style question below. **You don't need to answer this question.** Instead, think about what it is asking you to do, then answer Question 3.

Paper ②

7 **(a)**   The two texts are about the role of women in society.
   What similarities do both texts share about roles for women?
   Use evidence from both texts to support your answer.   **(6 marks)**

 3   Look at the short extracts below. Which quotation would you choose as part of your answer to Question 7 (a)? Circle one extract from each text.

(a) Extracts from *I am Malala*:

(i) In my old school, I was considered 'the smart girl'.
(ii) ... they know they have a great opportunity to fulfil their dreams of helping their communities.

(b) Extracts from 'Freedom or death':

(i) No man was ever put out of a public meeting for asking a question.
(ii) That is the history of humanity right from the beginning.

Synthesising evidence

In Paper 2, your ability to handle two texts together will be tested. Question 7 (a) will test AO1(b) and Question 7 (b) will assess AO3.

Read the exam-style question below. **You don't need to answer this question**. Instead, think about what it is asking you to do, then answer Questions 1 and 2.

> To show your full understanding of the synthesis question, you should start with an overview that sums up the main points of your answer.

Paper ②

> 7 (a) The two texts are about the role of women in society.
> What similarities are there between them in <u>considering</u> the role of women in society?
> Use evidence from both texts to support your answer. **(6 marks)**

1 Look at the student overview sentence below. Circle or underline the key words from the question that the student has included in their response. One has been done for you.

> Both writers <u>consider</u> the role of women in society: one writes about the right to vote, the other writes about access to education.

> Use key words from the question in your overview. This shows that the response will be relevant.

 2 Read the full extracts of 'Freedom or death' on page 100 and *I am Malala* on page 105. Find short quotations from the extracts to help support the student's overview used in Question 1.

> Use evidence from both texts to support your points.

....

....

....

 3 Read the concluding paragraph of the student response below.

(a) Underline all the linking phrases or adverbials the student has used in their response.

> Using linking phrases and suitable adverbials will help you to make the connections between the two texts and draw your ideas together.

> Emmeline Pankhurst seeks 'enfranchisement of women' so that they can play an active role in politics. Similarly, Malala and her friends want the opportunities to help 'their communities'. Both texts suggest that there are places in society where women should have equal access, for one this is politics and for the other it is education. In both texts, the writers believe that they have something to contribute to society.

(b) Now write one more sentence to add to the student's response.

....

....

....

> Try to make each sentence cover both texts. Use short quotations where possible and paraphrase text if quotation is too long.

Looking closely at language

Read these short extracts from *Notes from a Small Island*, then complete Questions 1 to 3.

Extract 1

> The only thing to be said for Bournemouth is that you are certainly spoiled for choice with hotels. Among the many gleaming palaces of comfort that lined every street for blocks around, I selected an establishment on a side-street for no good reason other than that I rather liked its sign: neat capitals in pink neon glowing beckoningly through the slicing rain.

Extract 2

> I'd lived in Bournemouth for two years and thought I knew it reasonably well, but the area around the station had been extensively rebuilt, with new roads and office blocks and one of those befuddling networks of pedestrian subways that compel you to surface every few minutes like a gopher to see where you are. By the time I reached the East Cliff, a neighbourhood of medium-sized hotels perched high above a black sea, I was soaked through and muttering.

> When you are looking closely at language and structure in two texts, remember to focus on:
> * connotations created by the writer (and the effect created)
> * literary or rhetorical devices the writer has chosen (and their effect)
> * types and lengths of sentences
> * the structure the writer has used.

1 Look at the words and phrases underlined in Extract 1. What are the connotations of the words and phrases? The first one has been done for you.

‘The only thing to be said’ suggests that there is little to say about Bournemouth.

‘for no good reason’ ....

....

 2 Write a sentence explaining the effect created by the words and phrases underlined in the extract. Include quotations and make sure you refer to their connotations.

....

....

3 Look at the language and sentence structure in the extract above.

(a) Identify a rhetorical device used and write a sentence commenting on the effect it creates.

The use of the simile ‘like a gopher’ suggests ....

....

(b) Explain the effect created by the sentence structure.

....

....

> In Paper 2, Question 7 (b) will ask you to compare two texts. When writing a comparison, always make a comparison point about each text, looking for both similarities and differences. Try to give the texts equal weighting in your answer.

> For Question 7 (b), you would identify any rhetorical devices used and compare them. In one it may be that the writer uses metaphors and similes, in another you may identify and comment on rhetorical questions and pattern of three. The uses of rhetorical devices will depend on the text type, audience and purpose.

Planning to compare

Read the short extracts 1 and 2 below, then answer Question 1.

Extract 1: from *I am Malala*

The school system here is very different from the one we had in Pakistan. In my old school, I was considered 'the smart girl'. I had this idea that I would always be the smartest one and that if I worked hard or not, I would always come first. Here in the UK, the teachers expect more from their students. In Pakistan, we used to write long answers. You really could write anything you liked; sometimes the examiners would get tired and give up reading part of the way through but still give you high marks! In England, the questions are often longer than the answers.

Extract 2: from 'Are fidget spinners a scam?'

Gerrell Knighsthead, an elementary school PE teacher in Paso Robles, California, posted a picture of fidget spinners on Twitter, writing: 'If another one of my students brings one of these to class I'm gonna lose my mind #teacherstruggles #fidgetspinner.' In response to the emergence of the new toy, some schools have banned them from being used in classrooms.
Kate Ellison, principal of Washington Elementary School in Evanston, Illinois, where the toys have been banned, told the *Chicago Tribune*: 'Frankly, we've found the fidgets (spinners) were having the opposite effect of what they advertise.
'Kids are trading them or spinning them instead of writing.'

1   Now look at the plan below, started by a student for comparing the language in the two texts and its effects. The plan is incomplete. Add as many details as you can, such as quotations and notes for explanations.

	Extract 1	**Extract 2**
Tone	neutral, informative, humorous	frustrated, irritated ....
Rhetorical devices/language	Formal, use of anecdote. For example, ...	Colloquial language such as, ...
Sentence structure	....	....

When comparing, you can:
• start with the language and structural techniques the texts have in common, then compare effects created **or**
• start with similarities in the effects created by the two texts (for example, tone) then compare the techniques the writers have used to create these effects.

Comparing ideas and perspectives

Read the openings to *I am Malala* on page 105 and 'Guidance from the Past' on page 103, then answer Question 1.

1 Finish this sentence, identifying and comparing the main ideas in the two openings.

Both texts start by expressing ideas about ....

....

Now read these short extracts below. Then answer Question 2.

Extract 1: *I am Malala*

(21st)

> He gets up first every day and prepares breakfast for me, my mother and my brothers Atal and Khushal.

Extract 2: 'Guidance from the Past'

> *Get out of your dream world and develop a backbone, not a wishbone, and start acting like an adult.*

> In Paper 2, you will need to answer 7 (a) and 7 (b) which are about both texts. 7 (a) asks you to look for **similarities**, synthesising ideas from both texts, while 7 (b) refers to **differences** as well as similarities.

2 Take a look at this task which is preparation for answering Question 7 (a).

Extract 1 suggests that the father has taken the role of catering for his children. How does this compare with Burville's perspective in Extract 2? Use evidence from Extract 2 in your answer.

> Write key points showing how Extract 1 compares with Extract 2.

Unlike the father in *I am Malala*, Burville believes that children should ....

....

....

....

Now read the full extracts. Pay particular attention to the way they end. Then answer Question 3.

Guided

3 Plan a P–E–E paragraph comparing the writers' ideas and perspectives throughout the extracts. Use your answers to Questions 1 and 2 above and consider whether the writers' perspectives remain the same throughout.

Point	....	It is a good idea to look at the differences between the beginning and the end of a text when you are thinking about ideas and perspectives. This will help you to compare the structure of the texts.
Evidence	....	
Explain	....	

Answering a comparison question

When you compare two texts, you can write about:

What the texts are about:

> Both texts are about …

> Text 1 is about …

> On the other hand, Text 2 explores …

The perspective:

> The writers' points of view (or other views they are presenting in their texts)

> The writer of Text 1 feels …

> The language in Text 1 suggests that …

> The perspective is positive/negative and shown through …

The effect on the reader:

> Both texts engage the reader …

> Text 1 uses humour whereas Text 2 uses …

Similar language features:

> Both texts use rhetorical devices: figurative language, pattern of three, questions, emotive language

> Text 1 poses a question followed by the answer (hypophora) …

> Text 2 uses a rhetorical question to …

> Remember to make direct comparisons of content as well as looking at the similarities and differences between the texts.

> **Guided**

1 Read the full extracts from *I am Malala* on page 105 and 'Guidance from the Past' on page 103. Use the prompts above to write a paragraph comparing the different ways language and structure are used for effect in these extracts. Remember to use quotations to support your points.

....

....

....

....

....

....

....

....

....

....

Putting it into practice

1 Read the full extracts from *I am Malala* on page 105 and 'Guidance from the Past' on page 103, then answer the exam-style question below.

Paper ②

7 **(b)** Compare how the writers of *I am Malala* and 'Guidance from the Past' present their ideas and perspectives on teenagers and their parents.

Support your answer with detailed reference to the texts.

(14 marks)

> When you tackle this type of question in the exam, remember to:
> - spend about 14 minutes on your answer
> - read the question carefully and highlight the main focus
> - spend a couple of minutes planning your answer before you start writing
> - refer to the whole text to find points relevant to the question
> - always write about both texts throughout your answer
> - identify the language and structural techniques used and comment on how they help the writer to get across their ideas and viewpoints.

....

....

....

....

....

....

....

....

....

....

....

....

....

....

....

....

....

....

....

....

....

> **Remember:** You have more space than this to answer your question in the exam. Use your own paper to finish your answer to the question above.

Evaluating a text

Both papers require you to evaluate a text. The phrase in both Paper 1 and Paper 2 is 'Evaluate how successfully this is achieved', which is meant to guide you to make judgements.

> The following synonyms also mean 'evaluate': form an opinion of, analyse, assess, judge, weigh up.

1 Here are the steps you will go through when answering an evaluation question. These have been jumbled up. Write them in the correct order in the boxes below.

- Read the text
- Write your answer
- Annotate key quotations
- Plan your answer
- Read the question

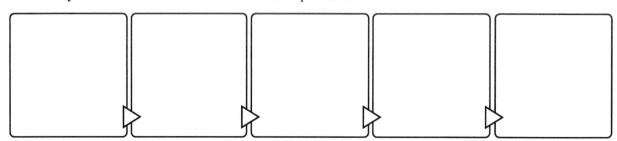

2 When you approach an evaluation question, you should identify any **ideas**, **events**, **themes** and **settings** that are relevant to the question.

 Paper ①

Draw lines to match the evaluative areas to their descriptions.

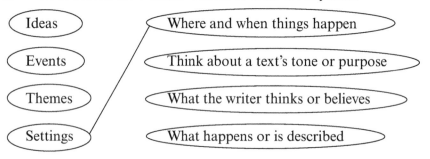

Ideas	Where and when things happen
Events	Think about a text's tone or purpose
Themes	What the writer thinks or believes
Settings	What happens or is described

> Consider all four evaluative areas when you read an extract, but only write about them if they are relevant. For example, setting may not be relevant for a non-fiction text.

3 Complete the table below, describing your approach to the two exam-style questions. **You do not need to answer the exam-style questions**. Look again at how each question is phrased and think about the amount of time you should spend on each one.

> For each question, remember that Assessment objective 4 – 'Evaluate texts critically and support this with appropriate textual references' – is being assessed.

 Paper ① ②

4 In this extract, there is an attempt to present the narrator as an imaginative storyteller. Evaluate how successfully this is achieved. Support your views with detailed reference to the text. **(15 marks)**	6 Bill Bryson attempts to engage the reader with descriptions of his experiences in Bournemouth. Evaluate how successfully this is achieved. Support your views with detailed reference to the text. **(15 marks)**
How long to spend on answer:	**How long to spend on answer:**
Focus of question:	**Focus of question:**
I'll need to look at (tick the best option): • an effect that is created in the extract • one specific aspect of the extract.	**I'll need to look at (tick the best option):** • an effect that is created in the extract • one specific aspect of the extract.

> Think about how the theme, setting, language and structure are used by the writer to achieve the desired effect. For example, in the Paper 1 question, you are evaluating the attempt to present the narrator as an imaginative storyteller, whereas in the Paper 2 question, you are evaluating how well the writer engages the reader with his descriptions of his experiences in Bournemouth.

Evaluating a text: fiction

Read the exam-style question below. **You don't need to answer this question**. Instead, think about what it is asking you to do, then answer Questions 1, 2 and 3.

Paper
①

> **4** In this extract there is an attempt to present Heathcliff as a negative influence in the house.
> Evaluate how successfully this is achieved.
> Support your views with detailed reference to the text.   **(15 marks)**

> Think about the assessment objective (AO4) being assessed. You need to 'evaluate' and this means making judgements.

1 Circle and annotate the extract from *Wuthering Heights* below as if you were preparing to answer the exam-style question. You should look for uses of setting, character, themes and language that present Heathcliff as a negative influence in the house.

> So, from the very beginning, he bred bad feeling in the house; and at Mrs Earnshaw's death, which happened in less than two years after, the young master had learnt to regard his father as an oppressor rather than a friend, and Heathcliff as a usurper of his father's affections, and his privileges, and he grew bitter with brooding over these injuries. I sympathised awhile, but, when the children fell ill of the measles, and I had to tend them, and take on me the cares of a woman at once, I changed my ideas.

emphasises how powerful and negative the very first impact Heathcliff had is.

2 Complete the following P–E–E paragraph about the setting in the short extract above. Add appropriate evidence, using your answer to Question 1, and explain how this builds up an impression of Heathcliff.

The setting successfully creates a negative impression of Heathcliff, as in the opening line his

influence on the house is described as breeding 'bad feeling' which ....

....

....

Now read the full extract for *Wuthering Heights* on page 99. Consider how events are used for effect.

3 Note at least three events which suggest that Heathcliff has a negative effect on life in the house. Add why or how you think these events reinforce how much of an impact Heathcliff has.

(a) ....

(b) ....

(c) ....

4 Now use the events you have listed for Question 3 to write a P–E–E paragraph, evaluating how successfully the writer presents Heathcliff as a negative influence.

....

....

....

....

....

....

> Settings and events are usually most relevant in a fiction text, but the ideas and themes are very important too.

Evaluating a text: non-fiction

Read this short extract from the opening of 'Freedom or death'. Look at how ideas and themes are used to engage the reader.

> Your forefathers decided that they must have representation for taxation, many, many years ago. When they felt they couldn't wait any longer, when they laid all the arguments before an obstinate British government that they could think of, and when their arguments were absolutely disregarded, when every other means had failed, they began by the tea party at Boston, and they went on until they had won the independence of the United States of America.

Idea: to be represented is important.

Now read the exam-style question below. **You don't need to answer this question**. Instead, think about what it is asking you to do, then answer Question 1.

Paper 2

> **6** The writer attempts to persuade the audience that actions can be justified to get results. Evaluate how successfully this is achieved.
> Support your views with detailed reference to the text.   **(15 marks)**

> When answering Question 6, Paper 2, remember that AO4 is being assessed so you will need to evaluate.

1 Have a look at the opening of the extract above. Identify the main ideas in this opening which would be useful when answering an exam-style Question 6. Annotate the extract, underlining evidence and ideas. One has been done for you.

Now read this short extract, also from 'Freedom or death'. Think about the themes in the extract, then answer Question 2.

> Themes are similar to ideas: they are the tone or purpose of the text. Ideas and themes are more likely to be in a non-fiction text. However, some non-fiction texts have events and settings.

> When you have warfare things happen; people suffer; the non-combatants suffer as well as the combatants. And so it happens in civil war. When your forefathers threw the tea into Boston Harbour, a good many women had to go without their tea.

2 One way to engage the reader is to use humour. Underline evidence of humour in the short extract above.

Now read the full extract of the speech on page 100 and answer Questions 3 and 4.

3 As it is a speech, the writer uses other events and devices to present her views. Make a list of those events and devices in the extract.

....

....

4 Write a P–E–E paragraph evaluating how successful the writer is in presenting her arguments. You could use some of your answers to Questions 1, 2 and 3 in your paragraph.

....

....

....

....

Putting it into practice

Guided

1 Read the full extract of *Middlemarch* on page 97, then answer the exam-style question below.

Paper
①

4 In this extract there is an attempt to present the different attitudes of Mary, Rosamond and Fred towards doing what is expected of them.
Evaluate how successfully this is achieved.
Support your views with detailed reference to the text. **(15 marks)**

> When you tackle this type of question you should:
> * spend around 30 minutes on your answer
> * read the question carefully and highlight the main focus
> * refer to the whole text, reading it thoroughly and annotating as you read
> * look at how ideas, events, themes and settings are used to create effects
> * use inference and evidence from the text to explain your ideas and assess how successfully this is achieved.

....

....

....

....

....

....

....

....

....

....

....

....

....

....

....

....

....

....

....

....

....

....

....

> **Remember**: You have more space than this to answer your question in the exam. Use your own paper to finish your answer to the question above.

Putting it into practice

 Guided

1 Read the extract from *I am Malala* on page 105, then answer the exam-style question below.

 Paper 1

4 In this extract there is an attempt to engage the reader by describing adapting to life in England. Evaluate how successfully this is achieved.

Support your views with detailed reference to the text.

(15 marks)

> When you tackle this type of question in the exam, remember to:
> • spend around 15 minutes on your answer
> • read the question carefully and highlight the main focus
> • refer to the whole text, reading it thoroughly and annotating as you read
> • look at how ideas, events, themes and settings are used to create effects
> • use inference and evidence from the text to explain your ideas and assess the effect of the text.

....

....

....

....

....

....

....

....

....

....

....

....

....

....

....

....

....

....

....

....

....

....

> **Remember**: You have more space than this to answer your question in the exam. Use your own paper to finish your answer to the question above.

Writing questions: an overview

Both GCSE English Language papers include a writing section: Section B.

1 Read the statements below. From your knowledge of the exam, decide which paper – or papers – each statement describes. Circle which paper each statement relates to. The first one has been done for you.

(a) The writing focus is imaginative writing.   **(Paper 1)   Paper 2   Both**

(b) The writing focus is transactional writing.   **Paper 1   Paper 2   Both**

(c) The writing section tests your ability to write for different audiences and purposes.   **Paper 1   Paper 2   Both**

(d) You will be given a choice of two tasks.   **Paper 1   Paper 2   Both**

(e) The writing tasks will be linked by theme to the reading extracts in Section A.   **Paper 1   Paper 2   Both**

Assessment objective 5

(a) Communicate clearly, effectively and imaginatively, selecting and adapting tone, style and register for different forms, purposes and audiences

(b) Organise information and ideas, using structural and grammatical features to support coherence and cohesion of texts

---

Assessment objective 6

Use a range of vocabulary and sentence structures for clarity, purpose and effect, with accurate spelling and punctuation

---

2 Now read these statements about the assessment objectives tested in the writing sections. Decide which of these assessment objectives is being described by the statements below. Circle your choices.

(a) Tests how well you can use sentences to structure and organise your writing effectively.   **AO5   AO6**

(b) Tests your vocabulary and whether you can use sentence structures for effect.   **AO5   AO6**

(c) Tests your spelling and punctuation.   **AO5   AO6**

(d) Tests your ability to write in different forms, for different purposes and audiences.   **AO5   AO6**

(e) Tests how well you can use paragraphs to structure and organise your writing effectively.   **AO5   AO6**

3 Summarise each assessment objective into one short sentence without using the words underlined above.

Assessment objective 5(a): ....

....

Assessment objective 5(b): Arrange ....

....

Assessment objective 6: ....

....

Writing questions: Paper 1

Paper 1 tests your imaginative writing skills.

1 Read the statements about Paper 1 below. Decide whether each statement is true or false.
   Circle your choices. One has been done for you.

   (a) The questions will tell you which form your writing should take.   **True** (**False**)

   (b) You should write in prose.   **True   False**

   (c) There will be two questions to choose from.   **True   False**

   (d) It is a good idea to plan your answer before you start to write.   **True   False**

Look at the exam-style questions below. **You don't need to answer these questions**. Instead, think about what they are asking you to do, then answer Questions 2 and 3.

Paper
1

5 Write about a time when someone made a significant impact on your life.
   Your response could be real or imagined.   **(40 marks)**

6 Look at images A and B on page 106.
   Write about a time when you, or someone you know, went on a special journey.
   Your response could be real or imagined. You may wish to base your response on one of the images.   **(40 marks)**

> There is a total of 40 marks available for the writing section of the paper:
> • a maximum of 24 marks are awarded for Assessment objective 5 (communication and organisation)
> • a maximum of 16 marks are awarded for Assessment objective 6 (spelling, punctuation, grammar and vocabulary).

2 Your imaginative writing does **not** have to be based on anything that has actually happened. Circle the phrase that makes this clear in both the exam-style questions.

3 Which word in Question 6 tells you that you do **not** have to base your writing on one of the images?

....

The table below shows three vital stages of answering a Paper 1 writing task.

4 Match up the stages below with the amount of time you should spend. The first one has been done for you.

   (a) Total time for Paper 1: Section B – Writing   30 minutes

   (b) Planning your answer   5 minutes

   (c) Writing your answer   45 minutes

   (d) Checking and proofreading* your answer   10 minutes

> *You will spend time on this later in the Workbook. It is very important to make time for checking your answer.

Writing questions: Paper 2

Paper 2 tests your skills in transactional writing.

1 Cross out the incorrect words or phrases from the pairs below. Two examples have been done for you.

Transactional writing is usually:

* formal / ~~informal~~
* intended to achieve a specific purpose / amusing and light-hearted
* entertaining and humorous / serious, with humour only if appropriate to the audience
* for a specific audience / suitable for all ages
* ~~open-ended~~ / carefully structured.

> There is a total of 40 marks available for the writing section of the paper:
> * a maximum of 24 marks are awarded for Assessment objective 5 (communication and organisation)
> * a maximum of 16 marks are awarded for Assessment objective 6 (spelling, punctuation, grammar and vocabulary).

Look at the exam-style questions below. **You don't need to answer these questions**. Instead, think about what they are asking you to do, then answer Question 2.

8 Write an article for your school magazine suggesting ways that the pressures of work could be reduced for Year 11 students.

In your article you could:

* state why pressures of work need to be addressed
* describe the role of revision clubs and revision classes
* suggest ways to reduce pressure in the future

as well as any other ideas you may have.

(40 marks)

9 Write a review of a place you have visited to post on a website as information for other visitors.

You could write about:

* the activities which were available
* who the place might appeal to
* whether or not you think that the place is worth a visit

as well as any other ideas you may have.

(40 marks)

2 (a) Circle the words in each question that tell you which **audience** you should be writing for.

(b) Circle the words in each question that tell you the **form** your writing should take.

(c) Circle the words in each question that tell you, or suggest to you, the **purpose** of your writing.

3 You have a total of 45 minutes for the Writing section in Paper 2. Complete the table by writing in the timings for each stage of your answer. One has been done for you.

	Start writing at 11.00 am
Planning your answer	11.00 –11.10
Writing your answer	
Checking and proofreading your answer	

> Don't forget to give yourself time to both plan and check your answer.

Writing for a purpose: imaginative

Look at the exam-style question below. **You don't need to answer this question**. Instead, think about what it is asking you to do, then answer Questions 1–4.

Paper
①

5 Write about a time when you, or someone you know, had an unusual encounter.
Your response could be real or imagined.

(40 marks)

1 Using the senses can help you to create a vivid picture in the reader's mind of what is being experienced. Complete the table below to gather ideas on how to use the senses for the exam-style question above. An idea has been added for you.

It looked like it would be any other day as I walked to the bus stop, until ...

see	
hear	I heard the sound of rustling in the hedge.
smell	
touch	
taste	

> A 'golden rule' of creative writing is to use verbs that **show**, rather than **tell**, the reader. For example, 'He shivered all over' is more interesting to read than 'He was cold'.

2 Rewrite the example sentence for the sense 'hear' to improve it.

....

3 The exam-style question above could be answered in the first person, which allows you to describe feelings in detail. Finish this sentence about how you were feeling:

I was very curious about what was making the noise: it was . . . .

....

> If you had used a third-person narrative voice you might have written: 'She was very curious, but would be even more curious later.' Using third person means you can use techniques such as foreshadowing.

4 Figurative language will help you make your writing more engaging. Use these figurative devices to describe three things that happen in the unusual encounter (such as appearance, movement or sounds).

Simile: It sounded like ....

Metaphor: ....

Personification: ....

> **Remember**: a simile says something is **like** something else, a metaphor says it **is** something else, and personification gives **living features** to an inanimate object.

5 Write the first three sentences of your answer to the exam-style question above. Use your answers from Questions 1–3 in your writing.

....

....

....

....

Writing for a purpose: inform, explain, review

Look at the exam-style question below. **You don't need to answer these questions**. Instead, think about what they are asking you to do, then answer Questions 1 to 4.

8 Write an information guide for students on an exchange visit to your school from another part of the country.

In your guide you could:

- give information about the school and its facilities, including sports and catering
- describe the local area and surrounding countryside/towns/villages
- suggest places to visit and things to do locally

as well as any other ideas you might have.

(40 marks)

1 Think about the audience for this piece of writing. What tone do you think would be appropriate? Use the words below to help you.

| serious | instructive | casual | informative | humorous | persuasive |

2 Transactional writing is structured so that information can be easily found. List up to four subheadings that you could use to organise your answer to the question above. An example has been done for you.

(a) ....

(b) ....

(c) ....

(d) What to do and see in the area

3 When you include facts and statistics, you need them to be relevant and realistic. Explain why the following examples would not be very useful for Question 8.

(a) This school was voted the worst school in the country.

....

(b) 25% of people prefer camels to penguins.

....

(c) In this country, is it illegal for anyone to own a bicycle.

....

> Questions in Paper 2, Section B will be linked by theme to the reading texts, so you may be able to use some of the facts or statistics provided. You can also make some up, but they need to be believable and appropriate.

4 A student has written the opening to their answer. Rewrite it, focusing particularly on the tone.

> It's got a building that they stuck up for learning stuff, lush sports stuff inside and out, a great performing arts bit if you're into that, and loads of people turn up to use it. Some don't even go to the school! Over 100% of students use the leisure stuff at the weekend.

....

....

Writing for a purpose: argue and persuade

Look at the exam-style question below. **You don't need to answer this question**. Instead, think about what it is asking you to do, then answer Questions 1 to 4.

Paper ②

9 Write an article for a local newspaper exploring the issues around the council's proposal to close the local park and nature reserve in order to build more affordable housing.
You could write about:
• who uses the local park and nature reserve, e.g. parents with young children, schools
• reasons why local people believe that the park and nature reserve should be saved
• your thoughts about other locations for building houses
as well as any other ideas you might have.

(40 marks)

1 Decide how far you do or do not agree with the proposal in exam-style Question 9, then write a key point to support your point of view.

Point 1: ....

2 Write down a piece of evidence to support your point in Question 1.

Evidence for point 1: ....

> Evidence could be facts or statistics, but in this type of question, you are more likely to use your own personal experience. You could include an 'expert opinion', for example from a community action group, but it must be believable.

3 A counter-argument allows you to dismiss an opposing point of view. Write down a counter-argument to the point you made in Question 1 above.

Some people might feel ....

....

However, ...

....

4 Rhetorical devices can also strengthen your argument. Choose three rhetorical devices and rewrite your answer to Question 1.

rhetorical questions   direct address   repetition   lists   alliteration

contrast   pattern of three   emotive language   hyperbole

(a) ....

    ....

(b) ....

    ....

(c) ....

    ....

> **Rhetorical question**: a question that does not necessarily expect an answer
> **Alliteration**: two or more words close together that begin with the same sound
> **Pattern of three**: a trio of words or phrases used to highlight or exaggerate a point
> **Lists**: series of items or ideas, often used to highlight quantity or variety
> **Direct address**: talking directly to the reader
> **Contrast**: putting two opposite facts side by side for effect
> **Hyperbole**: exaggerated/over-the-top statements or claims
> **Emotive language**: words chosen to have an emotional impact
> **Repetition**: using the same word or phrase for emphasis

Writing for an audience

Some Paper 2 questions will clearly state the audience you should write for. Others may imply or hint at the audience. Look at the exam-style question below. **You don't need to answer these questions.** Instead, think about how you might respond, then answer Questions 1 and 2.

Paper
②

9 Write an article for a national newspaper exploring the idea that social media damages face-to-face relationships.
You could write about:
• different types of social media
• types of relationships people have on social media
• alternatives to communicating on social media
as well as any other ideas you might have.

(40 marks)

1 Describe the implied audience for this piece of writing. Include your thoughts on age and gender.

The audience is likely to be ....

> Remember to think about how wide the implied audience might be. Newspapers can be read by people of all ages.

Guided

2 Look at the following sentence. Does it have an appropriate tone and vocabulary for the audience you identified in Question 1? Rewrite it to improve it.

The way we are going, we are going to forget how to actually talk to each other with all this social media malarkey!

....

....

....

Now look at the exam-style question below. **You don't need to answer this question.** Instead, think about the language you might use in your response, then answer Question 3.

Paper
②

8 Write a report for the student council, in which you consider the advantages and disadvantages of school uniform.
In your report you could:
• describe the benefits of having a school uniform
• explain why some think school uniform is now old-fashioned
• give your opinion about school uniform
as well as any other ideas you might have.

(40 marks)

3 An answer to Question 8 has been started for you below. Add two sentences to this opening.

There has been a lot of discussion in our year about whether or not we should still wear

school uniform. A strong argument for keeping school uniform is linked with the cost of

designer wear and how some students would find it difficult to keep up with their more

wealthy peers. ....

....

....

Putting it into practice

Look at the exam-style question below. **You don't need to answer these questions.** Instead, think about how you might respond, then answer Questions 1 and 2.

Paper
①

5 Write about a time when you, or someone you know faced a fear and conquered it.
   Your response could be real or imagined.   **(40 marks)**

> When you tackle this type of question in the exam, remember to:
> • plan your time – you have 45 minutes for this question, including planning and checking
> • plan your writing – including ideas about narrative voice and language techniques
> • make sure you write in prose
> • make sure you keep to the same narrative voice throughout your writing.

1 Now complete the following:

   (a) Total time: 45 minutes

   (b) Planning time: .... minutes

   (c) Writing time: .... minutes

   (d) Checking time: .... minutes

   (e) Form: ....

   (f) Narrative voice: ....

2 Note down some ideas about language techniques you could use in your answer to the exam-style question.

   • First person – so the reader will know exactly how I'm feeling

   • ....

   • ....

   • ....

   • ....

   • ....

> You may prefer to use a spider diagram instead of bullet points. Whichever you use, make sure you don't spend too long planning your answer.

Guided 3 Pick two techniques from Question 2 and write an example sentence for each.

   (a) ....

   ....

   ....

   ....

   (b) ....

   ....

   ....

   ....

Putting it into practice

Read the exam style questions below. **You don't have to answer these questions**. Instead, think about what they are asking you to do, then complete the table.

Paper ②

8 Write a review of the new cinema complex which has recently opened in your area.
In your review you could:
- describe the quality of the screens, seats, facilities and members of staff
- give details of the range of films available and whether or not they are value for money
- give your opinion about the cinema complex, including whether or not you recommend it
as well as any other ideas you might have.   **(40 marks)**

Paper ②

9 Write an article for your school magazine, exploring the idea that gaming is a waste of skills and time.
You could write about:
- the increasing popularity of gaming
- whether gaming can improve someone's skills, expertise and imagination
- your opinion about the impact of gaming on interaction with other people, including non-gamers
as well as any other ideas you might have.   **(40 marks)**

> When you tackle these kinds of questions in the exam, remember to:
> - plan your time – you have 45 minutes for this question, including planning and checking
> - read the question carefully and identify the topics
> - annotate the questions to highlight the form, audience and purpose
> - plan your writing, including key features of form and purpose.

1 Plan a response to one of the exam-style questions above by adding notes into the spider diagram below.

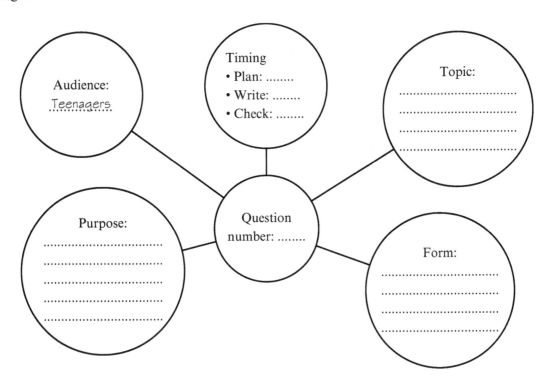

Form: articles and reviews

Read the exam-style question below. **You don't have to answer this question**. Instead, think about what it is asking you to do, then answer Questions 1 to 3.

Paper
2

9 Write an article for a local newspaper, exploring the idea that going to university is an essential life experience.

You could write about:
- the benefits of student life and improved employment prospects
- other life experiences being just as valuable
- how going to university is not suited for everyone, giving reasons, e.g. cost, some people preferring to go straight to work, other vocational paths

as well as any ideas you might have.

(40 marks)

1 Look at the proposed titles to use as a headline for this article. Pick which you think is the best one and explain why.

(a) Uni is a waste of time

(b) My article on whether or not I think it is a good idea to go to university

(c) University: essential or a luxury?

> Headlines use a range of techniques including rhetorical question, repetition, alliteration, a pun or a rhyme.

Headline .... is the best because ....

Guided

2 Think of a subheading that will add more information to your headline.

....

....

> Articles often quote reliable sources to back up any facts. For example, they might quote another newspaper or an expert to make the article more believable.

3 Look at the sources below and write some facts or quotations you could include as part of your article. The first one has been done for you.

(a) **Source:** Jan Mappin, senior psychologist in education

Quotation: 'While going to university might not be for everyone, those who can should,' argues Jan Mappin, senior psychologist in education. 'It isn't just the higher study, it's forming new friendships and responding to fresh challenges.'

(b) **Source:** A report from the National Union of Students

Fact: ....

4 In the exam, you may be asked to write a review. Look at this exam-style question. **You don't need to answer this question**. Instead, annotate it with any figurative language you might use in your response.

> Sometimes reviews use headlines and subheadings. In some cases, a review will be intended to entertain, so the writer might use more **figurative** language than in an article. For example, in your answer you can use:
> - senses   • simile   • metaphor   • personification.

Paper
2

The newly painted towers rose in the sky like ....

9 Write a review of a local theme park which has (recently reopened) after a full upgrade of facilities and additional new rides.

In your review you could:
- compare the old theme park with the (upgraded version) and give your opinion on any changes
- describe the facilities, including tickets, queues for rides
- give your opinion on whether or not there are major differences as well as any other ideas you might have.   **(40 marks)**

After months of eager anticipation

Form: letters and reports

Read the exam-style question below. **You don't have to answer this question.** Instead, think about what you might need to include in your response, then answer Question 1.

8 Write a letter to your local member of parliament in which you raise concerns that there are not enough leisure facilities in the area for young people.
In your letter you could:
- describe the current situation in your area concerning facilities for young people
- explain why you are concerned
- suggest ways to improve the situation
as well as any other ideas you might have.   **(40 marks)**

1 Part of a student's response is included below and the mistakes have been underlined. Sort the examples into the table below. One has been done for you.

Dear Sir/Madam,

Tons of old grumpies complain that young people hang around on the streets, making them feel uncomfortable. But you know what. I reckon there is nowhere else for them to go outside of school time. If more money was stuck into leisure facilities in the area then people could go there additionally, making them happier and also making the old windbags happier.

Yours sincerely,
Sophie Reynolds

Informal language	Incorrect use of word	Incorrect punctuation
reckon		

> If you are asked to write a letter in the exam, pay attention to tone and content. You should make it clear that you are writing a letter: begin with 'Dear' and end it appropriately.

Now read the exam-style question below. **You don't have to answer this question.** Instead, think about what you might need for this piece of writing, then answer Questions 2 and 3.

9 Write a report for your school newsletter about the successful visit of students from a different country.
You could write about:
- the length of the visit and how the school welcomed the guest students
- the activities and trips organised for them, including what went well
- the farewell assembly and possible plans for future projects
as well as any other ideas you might have.   **(40 marks)**

2 Reports need to be formal and factual. Write a suitable conclusion for the report in Question 9 that summarises the main facts about the topic.

....

3 Reports should inform their audience about a particular topic. They usually include recommendations or suggestions for ways forward. Look at the last bullet point in Question 9 and suggest two possible ways forward which could be used in your report.

(a) One possible project could be ....
....

(b) ....

57

Form: information guides

Read this exam-style question. **You don't need to answer the question**. Instead, think about what you might need to include in your response, then answer Questions 1 to 4.

Paper ②

8 Write an information guide for new students joining your school.

In your guide you could:
- describe the layout of the school and a typical school day
- give information about events in the school calendar year
- explain how they can get involved in clubs and after-school activities

as well as any other ideas you might have.

(40 marks)

1 Your information guide will need a heading or title to engage the reader. Write down three possible headings for the guide in Question 8 using techniques such as alliteration, a pun, or a pattern of three. One has been done for you.

(a) Students: Things to do, see and explore

(b) ....

(c) ....

Guided 2 Choose the best of your headings in Question 1 and explain why it would be the most effective for your school student audience.

....

....

3 Subheadings help to structure an information text and guide the reader. Write down two subheadings that you could use in your information guide for new students. An example has been done for you.

(a) What is a typical day like?

(b) ....

(c) ....

> Lists are a useful way to get across a large amount of information. They are often used at the start of an information guide to signpost to the reader what will be included in the guide.

Guided 4 What could you list at the start of your information guide for new students at your school? Write a list using no more than four bullet points.

....

....

> Lists can be numbered or in bullets but avoid using too many as you will be assessed on sentences, adverbials and paragraphs.

Guided 5 Now choose one bullet point above and write one or two detailed sentences to explain it further.

....

....

Putting it into practice

1 Answer the exam-style question below. Focus on audience, form and purpose.

9 Write a letter to your local newspaper, suggesting ways the high street could be improved.

In your letter you could:

- give your views on the high street as it is now, e.g. lack of shops, heavy traffic
- explain why the high street is important for the whole community
- explain the potential benefits of improving the high street

as well as any other ideas you might have.

(40 marks)

> When you tackle this type of question in the exam, remember to:
> - spend 45 minutes on your answer, including planning and checking time
> - read the question carefully and identify the topic
> - annotate the question to highlight the form, audience and purpose
> - plan your writing before you start
> - include all the relevant key features of the form and purpose.

....

....

....

....

....

....

....

....

....

....

....

....

....

....

....

....

....

....

....

....

> **Remember:** You have more space than this to answer your question in the exam. Use your own paper to finish your answer to the question above.

Prose: an overview

For Paper 1, you are required to produce imaginative writing and it is important that you use an appropriate form in your response.

1 In what form should you write your response for Paper 1: prose, poetry or a play? Explain your answer.

....

2 Look at the following list. For which of the options below is prose not the form usually used? Tick your choices.

    (a) narratives (stories)   (b) descriptions   (c) poems   (d) monologues

3 Write a brief definition of prose.

    Prose is continuous ....

....

4 Read the short extracts below. Match the extracts to the options: narrative, monologue or description.

    A He had a rich complexion, which verged on swarthiness[1], a flashing black eye, and dark, bushy brows and hair. When he indulged in an occasional loud laugh at some remark among the guests, his large mouth parted so far back as to show the rays of the chandelier a full score or more of the two-and-thirty sound white teeth that he could obviously still boast of.

1: *swarthiness* – a dark complexion

    B Hindley threw it, hitting him on the breast, and down he fell, but staggered up immediately, breathless and white; and, had I not prevented it, he would have gone just so to the master, and got full revenge by letting his condition plead for him, intimating who had caused it.

    C I did it again today; I forgot to bring my reusable shopping bags to the grocery store. Actually, I'm a little embarrassed that I didn't even think of them until my son gasped in horror and said, under his breath, 'Mom, she's putting our groceries in plastic!'

Narrative (tip: look for sequence of events)

Monologue (tip: look for a strong sense of voice)

Description (tip: look for sense of place or person)

In the exam, structure your ideas carefully and for effect. Your writing should have a clear beginning, middle and end. Use full paragraphs and avoid too much dialogue.

Ideas and planning: imaginative

Read these exam-style questions. **You don't need to answer these questions**. Instead, consider the two question options, then answer Questions 1 to 3.

Paper ①

5 Write about a time when you, or someone you know, really made a difference to a person in need. Your response could be real or imagined. **(40 marks)**

6 Look at the images on page 106.
Write about a journey with an important mission.
Your response could be real or imagined. You may wish to base your response on one of the images. **(40 marks)**

> **Guided**   1 In the exam you will need to choose a question quickly to save time for detailed planning. For which of the two questions above do you have some ideas? Circle your choice.

> **Guided**   2 In the space below, write down your initial ideas for your choice, either as a list or a spider diagram.

> Think about:
> • the scene or event in your mind (even if you chose an image)
> • the characters: thoughts, words and actions
> • sequence of writing.
> Use the question you have chosen as your focus and check that your ideas are centred on it.

3 Now look at the student's plan for Question 6 below. Add details to the plan, including any devices such as figurative language that you intend to use.

> Title: The mission: to visit great aunt at her house in the middle of nowhere
> *a diary or letter from relative that you need to deliver?*

⬇

> Description of journey – adjectives such as 'winding' road

⬇

> Finding the house

⬇

> Describe state of the house

> If you chose Question 6, you do not have to use the images. This means your mission could be very different and not necessarily involve 'winding' roads and abandoned buildings.

Structure: imaginative

> You need to be able to control your writing, which is particularly important in an exam when you have a limited amount of time. Use a narrative structure to order your ideas.

Read the exam-style question below. **You don't have to answer this question**. Instead, think about how you might structure an answer to this question, then answer Question 1.

Paper ①

5 Write about a time when you, or someone you know, realised that you had completely misjudged a person.
Your response could be real or imagined.

(40 marks)

1 Complete the narrative structure for a response to Question 5 below and remember to include appropriate imaginative-writing techniques as well as your own ideas.

> **Remember**: In narrative these terms describe specific functions:
> - **Exposition** – initial scene-setting/actions/events/story information and backstory. Be careful that you don't spend too long on the backstory so you mostly show rather than tell.
> - **Rising action** – this is the combination of events that build up to the next stage, known as the climax.
> - **Climax** – this is the turning point of the story, where actions/ideas reach their peak.
> - **Falling action** – this is where the writer brings things together/'ties up the loose ends' for the reader.
> - **Resolution** – this is the closure of the story/piece of writing.

Exposition: At first he appears a genuinely nice person, always cheerful and ....

....

Rising action: ....

> Use the senses: what does the narrator see, hear or smell as he/she approaches the place?

....

Climax: ....

> Use a metaphor or simile.

> Use dramatic adjectives or verbs.

....

Falling action: ....

....

Resolution: ....

....

Guided

2 You can play with narrative structure and change the order. Rewrite your plan, but this time, start at the climax and use flashbacks to tell the story.

Climax: ....

....

....

....

....

Resolution: ....

....

....

Beginnings and endings: imaginative

Your beginning needs to engage the reader immediately and set the tone for the rest of your writing. Look at this exam-style question. **You don't need to answer the question.** Instead, think about how you might begin and end an answer to this question, then complete Question 1 below.

Paper
①

> 5 Write about a time when you, or someone you know, had an embarrassing experience.
>   Your response could be real or imagined.   **(40 marks)**

1 You will need to start with some quick planning: Complete the list below to get started.

One-sentence description of the experience: ....

Narrative voice: .... (first/third person)

Who is involved? ....

Where is the story set? ....

> Listing some quick ideas before you start will help you feel more confident.

> Having these ideas in mind will help you to get started more easily.

2 Write several different beginnings in response to this exam-style question. One has been done for you, using vivid description.

> Don't be tempted to overuse dialogue. Mix it with plenty of prose to demonstrate your sentence structure skills.

Vivid description	Dialogue
It was a beautiful day, the weather was perfect and everyone seemed so happy. It all looked like everything would go to plan. All the signs were there that nothing could possibly go wrong.	
Experience/context	**Conflict**

The ending of a piece of imaginative prose is just as important as the opening. Choose one of your openings from Question 2, then answer Questions 3 and 4.

> Guided

3 Write a possible final sentence to your story.

....

....

> Guided

4 Rewrite your final sentence from Question 3 by changing the tone of the sentence. You can use any tone; for example, positive, negative or tense. Rewrite the sentence three times.

(a) ....

(b) ....

(c) ....

> Make sure your ending is as imaginative as possible and avoid endings such as 'it was just a dream'. This is very frustrating for the reader and suggests that the writer could not think of a good ending!

Putting it into practice

Read the exam-style question below. **You don't need to answer this question.** Instead, think of what you could write about, then answer Question 1.

Paper ①

5 Write about a time when you, or someone you know, had to cope with a new and challenging experience.

Your response could be real or imagined.

(40 marks)

> When you plan for this type of question in the exam, remember to:
> - spend 10 minutes on the detailed plan
> - plan for a clear narrative structure
> - plan the narrative voice and imaginative writing techniques you will use.

1 Use the space below to plan your answer to the exam-style question.

Ideas and planning: inform, explain, review

Read the exam-style question below. **You don't need to answer this question**. Instead, think about what it is asking you to do, then answer Question 1.

Paper ②

8 Write a review of a recent important event at your school.
In your review you could:
- give the background/history of the event, including how it all began
- describe the event, including what happened, who was there and how it ended
- explain how successful the event was for the school
as well as any other ideas you might have.

(40 marks)

> Use the bullet points in the question to support your planning.

1 Plan an answer to Question 8. Work through the planning stages below, then complete the plan. Some ideas have been added for you.

(a) Plan your introduction. Tell your reader what you are writing about and be engaging so that your readers will want to read on.

(b) You will need three or four key points. Decide which key points you will include and use the bullet points in the question as a guide for this.

(c) Add detail to each of your key points, including techniques appropriate to your audience and purpose.

(d) Number your key points in the sequence that you will use them in your writing. Which will work best at the beginning and which at the end?

(e) Plan your conclusion.

(f) Add ideas for temporal adverbials (such as later, soon, tomorrow, yesterday) to help guide your reader through points.

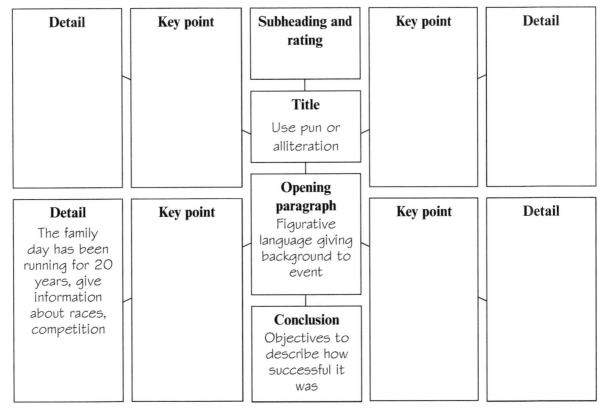

> It is worth taking the time to plan writing carefully, so that you can produce work of your best quality.

Ideas and planning: argue and persuade

Read the exam-style question below. **You don't need to answer the question.** Instead, think about what it is asking you to do, then answer Question 1.

Paper ②

9 Write an article for your school magazine, exploring the view that mobile phones should be banned in schools.

You could write about:
- whether or not mobile phones are a distraction in lessons
- the possible benefits of having mobile phones in schools
- the importance of having access to communication in today's society

as well as any other ideas you might have.

(40 marks)

1 Plan an answer to Question 9. Work through the planning stages as described below.

(a) Summarise your response as the starting point.

....

....

(b) Plan an introduction that tells readers what you are writing and why they should read it. First sentence:

....

....

....

(c) Decide on **three** key points that you want to make in your article. Add a piece of evidence to support each point. One has been done for you.

Point 1: Students need phones for emergencies/organising lifts.

Evidence: Last year 10% of buses were late or cancelled.

Point 2: ....

Evidence: ....

Point 3: ....

Evidence: ....

(d) Sequence your key points by numbering them in the order that you want to use them in your response. Think about what would be a logical order – you may find the bulleted points in the question a useful guide.

(e) Add a counter-argument. What might someone who disagrees with one of your points present as an argument? How can you dismiss their argument?

....

....

> You could present your plan as a spider diagram or simply as a list of bullet points. Use a way to plan that suits you.

(f) Write a concluding sentence.

....

....

> You only have 45 minutes to plan, write and check your answer. Aim for six paragraphs of well-crafted writing.

Openings: transactional

Read the exam-style question below. **You don't need to answer this question**. Instead, think about what it is asking you to do, then answer Questions 1 and 2.

Paper ②

9   Write an article for a local newspaper exploring the argument that internet access should be controlled for under 18-year-olds.

In your article you could write about:

• views for and against censorship (controlling what content can be seen/accessed)

• concerns about the safety of young people and children

• the disadvantages of internet control

as well as any other ideas that you might have.

(40 marks)

1   The first sentences of any writing are important because they need to grab the attention of the reader. Look at the following examples of opening sentences below. Underline the style of opening sentence that you think is the most effective. Explain the reasons for your choice.

Using a rhetorical question: Who would want to live in a world controlled by censorship?

Making a bold or controversial statement: Censorship is completely wrong. It should not be allowed as it is used to control the population.

With a relevant quotation: 'The internet is a dangerous place for young people and children, they need protecting.'

With a shocking or surprising fact or statistic: Many parents openly admit that they do not know what their children are looking at on the internet.

With a **short**, relevant, **interesting** anecdote: My friend lived in a country where the internet was controlled and it simply meant that she found it impossible to carry out research as she was prevented from accessing harmless material.

....

....

....

....

....

....

....

....

2   A student's opening paragraph is below. Cross out the text you think could be removed to make the start more interesting.

In this article, I am going to argue that internet access should not be controlled for under 18-year-olds. Would you feel comfortable talking to friends, going to work or even watching TV knowing that someone else was controlling what you did?

Don't tell the reader what you are going to be writing about – just write it!

Conclusions: transactional

Read the exam-style question below. **You don't need to answer this question**. Instead, think about what it is asking you to do, then answer Questions 1 and 2.

Paper ②

9 Write an article for a newspaper, exploring the issue of using animals for entertainment, such as circuses and sea-life centres.

You could write about:

- why there are concerns about using animals for entertainment
- whether or not animals are harmed in these situations
- alternative forms of entertainment that do not involve animals

as well as any other ideas you might have.

(40 marks)

1 The final paragraph or conclusion to your writing should make a lasting impression. Take a look at the example below where a student has referred back to their introduction in the concluding sentence.

So while it has been fun for many to see circus tricks or dolphins doing impressive stunts, we have a duty to treat animals with respect.

Now using the student answer as a guide, change the conclusion using the the techniques below.

End on a vivid image: To be able to see the majestic dolphins leaping with joy and freedom surely means the vast blue ocean is their rightful home.

End on a warning: ....

....

End on a happy note: ....

....

End on a thought-provoking question: ....

....

End on a 'call to action': ....

....

Guided **2** Which technique do you think is the most effective for your conclusion? Explain why you think this.

....

....

....

....

....

....

> Think about how you might sum up your whole argument neatly, leaving your reader with a clear message.

Putting it into practice

Read the exam-style question below. **You don't need to answer this question**. Instead, think about what it is asking you to do, then answer Question 1.

Paper
② 8 Write a review of a local festival or event which you have attended.
    In your review you could write about:
    • the type of festival or event you attended
    • the activities that took place
    • what makes this festival or event so successful
    as well as any other ideas you might have.
                                     (40 marks)

> When you plan for this type of question, remember to:
> • read the question carefully and identify the topic
> • identify the form, purpose and audience before you start
> • spend about 10 minutes planning your answer
> • plan the features and techniques you will use to support the form, audience and purpose
> • organise and sequence your ideas
> • plan your introduction and conclusion.

 Guided 1 Use the space below to plan your answer to Question 8 above.

Paragraphing for effect

Read the exam-style question below. **You don't need to answer this question.**

 Paper ②

9 Write an article for the school newsletter, exploring the idea that music, art and drama should be compulsory for all students up to Year 11.

In your article you could write about:
- the extra time these lessons would take
- the importance of arts subjects
- that optional after-school activities are available for these subjects

as well as any other ideas you might have.

(40 marks)

Now look at the paragraph below. It is from a student's response to the exam-style question above.

Many of us appreciate that music, art and drama enrich our lives but how these subjects could be included in our current, overcrowded curriculum is a major issue. We have full timetables now, so, short of extending the school day, the arts could only be included at the expense of other subjects. Also, would it be compulsory for all students to take these arts subjects at exam level?

The student has organised the paragraph using Point–Evidence–Explain.

1 Identify and label the three different sections of this paragraph: point, evidence and explain. One has been done for you.

Point: Many of us appreciate that music, art and drama enrich our lives but ....

....

Evidence: ....

Explain: ....

2 A student has written down some ideas in response to this exam-style question. Identify which are points, which are evidence, and which are explanation. An example is given below.

(a) Music, art and drama are more difficult to make careers from. ....

(b) There are more important subjects which should be concentrated on. ....

(c) Only 5% of universities ask for a qualification in arts   evidence

(d) Creative students would enjoy these subjects being compulsory. ....

(e) Students should be given lots of choice to suit their abilities. ....

(f) A subject such as maths is more useful in day-to-day life. ....

(g) Studies found that happier students had overall better grades. ....

> Guided > 3 Now choose a point, evidence and explanation from Question 2 to write your own answer.

....

....

....

> Guided > 4 Identify and label the three different sections of your paragraph: **point, evidence** and **explain**.

Each time you start a new point in an essay, start a new paragraph. If you are writing to inform, explain, or describe, then start each new paragraph with a topic sentence.

Linking ideas

Different adverbials have different purposes.

1 Copy the adverbials below into the table, adding each one to the correct column.

Consequently   ~~For example~~   For instance   Furthermore

However   On the other hand   In particular   In the same way

Similarly   Significantly   Therefore   Moreover

Adding an idea	Explaining	Illustrating	Emphasising	Comparing	Contrasting
		For example			

> Remember that time or temporal adverbials – such as afterwards, before, meanwhile – are useful ways to indicate the passage of time in imaginative writing.

> Your argument will be stronger if you use adverbials to link your points together.

Read the exam-style question below. **You don't need to answer this question**. Instead, think about what it is asking you to do, then answer Questions 2 and 3.

Paper ②

9 Write an article for the school magazine exploring the idea of banning all 'unhealthy' foods in school.

You could write about:

- which foods are considered unhealthy
- what the school might have to do if they impose the ban
- whether or not this is a good idea

as well as any other ideas you might have.

(40 marks)

2 Look at the paragraphs below. They are extracts from one student's response to Question 9. Fill in all the gaps using appropriate adverbials.

Quite often opinions change and experts decide that something considered healthy is unhealthy after all .... , natural fruit juices are thought to contain unhealthy levels of sugar because of the way they are processed. Take the egg as a case in point, as experts warned that eating too many would be bad for us, ... we should restrict our intake. Now, this warning is rarely heard.

There are all sorts of issues concerning the school bringing in such a ban. In reality, this would be difficult to enforce .... would the school be exceeding its powers and interfering with family decisions? .... does the school have the moral right?

3 Now write your own Point–Evidence–Explain paragraph in response to Question 9 above. Remember to use a range of adverbials to guide the reader through your argument.

....

....

....

> Look back at the planning activities to help you.

Putting it into practice

1 Answer the exam-style question below. Focus in particular on your uses of paragraphs and adverbials.

9 Write an article for a magazine exploring the idea that some prison sentences should be replaced by community service.

You could write about:

• the sorts of jobs people could do, e.g. gardening, painting and decorating, improving parks
• how this would benefit the community
• how offenders may benefit more from doing community service than by spending time in prison

as well as any other ideas you might have.   **(40 marks)**

> When you tackle any writing question in the exam, remember to:
> • write in paragraphs
> • plan one main idea for each paragraph
> • use P–E–E to structure your paragraph
> • organise and sequence your paragraphs
> • use adverbials to link your paragraphs and guide your reader through your ideas.

....

....

....

....

....

....

....

....

....

....

....

....

....

....

....

....

....

....

....

> **Remember:** you have more space than this to answer your question in the exam. Use your own paper to finish your answer to the question above.

Vocabulary for effect: synonyms

Synonyms are words with similar meanings. You can use a range of different words with similar meanings to avoid repetition and add variety to your writing, but do make sure that the vocabulary you choose works in the context of your sentence.

1 Look at the sentence below. Think of **at least two** synonyms for each circled word.

Synonyms for 'extra':

1 more

2 ....

Synonyms for 'significant':

1 ....

2 ....

(Extra) revision (classes) can make (significant) differences to examination (outcomes).

Synonyms for 'classes':

1 ....

2 ....

Synonyms for 'outcomes':

1 ....

2 ....

Although you can use a thesaurus, try to think of the synonyms yourself as you won't have a thesaurus in the exam!

2 Look at each of the words in the table below. Complete the table by adding at least two synonyms for each word. An example has been done for you.

angry	happy	shout	anxious	confident
			fretful apprehensive nervous	

Look at the exam-style question below. **You don't need to answer this question**. Think about what you might include in a response and answer Question 3.

Paper ①

5 Write about a time when you, or someone you know, had a disagreement with someone in authority. Your response can be real or imagined.   **(40 marks)**

Guided

3 Write the beginning of your response to the above exam-style question. Use some of the vocabulary from Question 2 in your writing and make it as dramatic as possible.

....

....

....

Guided

4 Now rewrite your response to the exam-style question above. This time, choose synonyms that make it seem as uninteresting as possible.

....

....

....

Vocabulary for effect: argue and persuade

Emotive words are important when you are writing to argue or persuade, because you are hoping to convince your reader.

1 Look at the sentences below. Circle or highlight the emotive language in each sentence which is used to add more impact. One has been done for you.

(a) People waste an (excessive) amount of time on social media with disastrous consequences.

(b) If we continue to ignore drastic climate change, we will be in serious trouble.

(c) We can be unnecessarily horrible to our pets and treat them very cruelly.

 2 Look at this sentence:

> Some parents are unhappy about the school's plan to ban unhealthy food from the school's premises.

Rewrite the sentence three times using different emotive language to add more impact.

(a) ....

....

(b) ....

....

(c) ....

....

Look at the exam-style question below. **You don't need to answer this question.** Instead, think about what you might include in a response to this question then answer Question 3.

Paper ②

9 Write an article for the local newspaper exploring the issues of litter and vandalism in the town centre.
You could:
- describe the problem
- explain why it is a problem
- suggest possible solutions

as well as any other ideas you might have.   **(40 marks)**

 3 Write two sentences in response to Question 9 above. Aim to choose vocabulary for its impact and its connotations.

....

....

....

....

....

....

Language for different effects 1

You can add power and impact to your writing by using a range of language techniques.

1 Here is an example sentence. Rewrite the sentence using contrast, repetition, a rhetorical question and a list. One has been done for you.

> The town square was very busy.

Contrast: ....

Repetition: ....

Rhetorical question: Who would want to be crammed in there with everyone else?

List: ....

Guided 2 Which language technique do you think has the best effect? Explain your answer.

....

....

....

Look at the exam-style question below. **You don't need to answer this question**. Instead, think about the language techniques you might include in a response and answer Question 3.

Paper ② 8 Write a letter to your local animal rescue centre, applying to do voluntary work at weekends. In your letter you could:
  • describe any experience you have working with animals
  • explain why this voluntary work appeals to you
  • explain why you admire the work that the animal rescue centre does

as well as any other ideas you might have. **(40 marks)**

Guided 3 Pick one of the language techniques explored in Question 1 and use it to write a paragraph of your answer to the exam-style Question 8.

....

....

....

....

....

....

....

....

....

....

....

Had a go ☐ Nearly there ☐ Nailed it! ☐

Language for different effects 2

You can add power and impact to your writing by using a range of language techniques.

1 Look at the extracts from the students' writing below. Some are taken from an imaginative piece of writing, some from a piece of transactional writing. Connect the rhetorical techniques to the extracts. An example has been done for you.

A
She was spilling so much as she poured it, she might as well have tipped it straight on to the floor.

B
Have you ever done something that you regretted immediately?

C
The student slithered, sneaked and slunk out of the classroom.

Direct address

Pattern of three

Alliteration

Hyperbole

D
I could see the large creature advancing in the fog, lumbering, bumbling and hulking.

E
If you think you could do better, go ahead and try!

F
I must have told her a thousand times that I would not be going to the revision class.

> Think about which sentence grabs your attention, and **why** it makes you want to read on.

 2 Which language technique do you think is most effective? Explain your answer.

....

....

Look at the exam-style question below. **You don't need to answer this question**. Instead, think about what you might include in a response to this question then answer Question 3.

Paper ② 8 Write a review of a new school building that contains eating and social areas, which has recently been opened by the local Member of Parliament.
In your review you could:
• explain why the new block was built
• describe how it compares with what was there before
• decide whether or not you think it is value for money
as well as any other ideas you might have.

(40 marks)

 3 Start your answer to Question 8 above. Use one or more of the language techniques explored in Question 1.

....

....

....

....

....

....

....

Language for different effects 3

Figurative language can be used to create powerful images in the mind of the reader.

1 Read the examples of **similes**, **metaphors** and **personification** below. Change each sentence to another type of figurative language. The first one has been done for you.

(a) Simile: Talking to her is like talking to a brick wall.

Metaphor: She is a brick wall when you talk to her

(b) Metaphor: Learning anything is a slippery slope: you think you are getting there and you slide back down again.

Simile: ....

(c) Personification: The moon crept into every garden, creating soft lighting.

Simile: ....

(d) Personification: The cover of the exam paper teases us and asks: 'Do you want to see inside?'

Metaphor: ....

(e) Metaphor: The staircase was a vast mountain that reached to the sky.

Personification: ....

(f) Simile: Moving quietly, she slid like a snake and no-one noticed her leave.

Metaphor: ....

> A **simile** compares one thing to another, often using 'like' or 'as'.
> A **metaphor** says one thing is another to create comparison.
> **Personification** gives non-human objects human characteristics.

Look at the exam-style question below. **You don't need to answer this question**. Instead, think about the figurative language you might include in a response and answer Question 2.

Paper ①

5 Write about a time when you, or someone you know, had to keep a dreadful secret. Your response can be real or imagined.

(40 marks)

> Guided

2 Write up to four short examples from an answer to Question 5 above. Use one of the figurative devices explored in Question 1 in each example.

....

....

....

....

....

....

....

....

....

> Don't overuse figurative language in your answers. If you are selective, the ones you do use will have more impact.

Using the senses

Look at the examples of descriptive language used in the extracts below. The writer has used the five senses to engage the reader and make descriptions more vivid.

A   There were traces of a delicate floral scent carried in on the breeze.

B   I could feel the cold grey mist rolling in from the sea.

C   Footsteps clattered loudly and suddenly on the flagstones.

D   The taste of salt was strong in the sea air.

E   I could see a flicker in the distance but, as it grew nearer, it became a huge and menacing beast.

⟩Guided⟩   **1** Circle the extract that you feel is **not** particularly effective.

> Avoid starting sentences with 'I could smell' or 'I saw' – imaginative writing is better if you **show**, rather than **tell**.

⟩Guided⟩   **2** Why is the example you have chosen not very effective?

....

....

⟩Guided⟩   **3** Which example is the most effective in Question 1? Explain why.

....

Look at the exam-style question below. **You don't need to answer this question**. Instead, think about what you might include in a response and answer Question 4.

Paper ①

5 Write about a time when you or someone you know was in the wrong place at the wrong time. Your response may be real or imagined.   **(40 marks)**

4 Write the opening paragraph of a response to this exam-style question. The start has been done for you. Try to:

• use one sense other than sight

• include an example of figurative language (such as similes, metaphors and personification).

He had no idea how he had got there. This was a strange, desolate place and he broke into a sweat when he realised he was not alone. There, on the horizon, a mountainous mass was moving towards him, the shrill shrieks pierced the air and echoed around him. ....

....

....

....

....

> Don't try and use every type of figurative language in your answers. Be selective and look for opportunities to add impact to your ideas.

Narrative voice

Below is an extract written in the first person.

> I know I am supposed to be disappointed and everyone thinks I am 'putting a brave face on it'. The truth? I am so relieved, you have no idea!

1 Rewrite the extract above in the third person or omniscient third person.

> **Remember:**
> • A third-person narrator uses 'he' and 'she'.
> • An omniscient third-person narrator can see into any character's mind.
> • First person narration uses 'I' and 'we' and can help the reader to feel very close to your main character.

....

....

....

....

Look at the exam-style question below. **You don't need to answer this question**. Instead, think about how you might start your response and answer Question 2.

**Paper
①**

5 Write about a time when you, or someone you know, explored an abandoned house. Your response could be real or imagined.   **(40 marks)**

2 Write two possible openings to this exam-style question. Use a different narrative voice for each opening and aim to write two or three sentences each time.

(a) I approached along the path warily, ...

....

....

....

....

....

....

(b) ....

....

....

....

....

....

....

Putting it into practice

 1 Answer the exam-style question below. Focus in particular on your use of language and language techniques for effect.

 8 Write a report to go into the school newsletter exploring the highs and lows of the academic year you have just finished.
You could:
- describe the good things that happened during the year (for example, a successful fund-raising event)
- explain why some events or times of the year were more of a challenge
- suggest different approaches for the next academic year

as well as any other ideas you might have.

(40 marks)

> When you tackle any writing question in the exam, you should think about language. Remember to:
> - annotate the question to highlight the form, audience and purpose
> - choose language that is appropriate for the audience and purpose
> - choose language techniques with care and for impact
> - avoid using too many techniques – it is more important that your writing is well-structured and appropriate for the audience and purpose.

....

....

....

....

....

....

....

....

....

....

....

....

....

....

....

....

> **Remember:** You have more space than this to answer your question in the exam. Use your own paper to finish your answer to the question above.

Putting it into practice

Guided 1 Write a response to the exam-style question below. Focus in particular on your use of language and language techniques for effect.

Paper ① 5 Write about a time when you, or someone you know, accidentally broke the rules.
Your response can be real or imagined.   **(40 marks)**

> When you tackle any writing question in the exam, you should think about the language. Remember to:
> * choose language that is appropriate for your audience
> * make ambitious and effective vocabulary choices to engage your reader
> * use a range of language techniques
> * avoid using too many examples of simile, metaphor or personification – a few original ideas are better than a mass of clichés.

....
....
....
....
....
....
....
....
....
....
....
....
....
....
....
....
....
....
....
....
....
....
....

> **Remember:** You have more space than this to answer your question in the exam. Use your own paper to finish your answer to the question above.

Sentence variety 1

Using a range of different sentence types can help you to convey your ideas clearly and engage the reader.

1 A student wrote the sentence below:

> She read her book.

This sentence is a single-clause sentence.
Rewrite the sentence using the following different sentence types. One has been done for you.

(a) A multi-clause sentence with a subordinate clause ....

....

(b) A multi-clause sentence with a coordinate clause ....

....

(c) A multi-clause sentence with a relative clause ....

....

(d) A minor sentence

> 'Book reader!'

Look at the exam-style question below. **You don't need to answer this question**. Think about how you might use different sentence types in your response.

Paper ②

> **9** Write an article for a national newspaper exploring the idea that celebrities should be allowed more privacy by the press.
> You could:
> • describe the possible jobs of celebrities
> • explain how a celebrity's privacy might be invaded
> • suggest ways to give celebrities more privacy.
> as well as any other ideas you might have.
>
> **(40 marks)**

Now consider this extract from one student's answer to Question 9, then answer Question 2.

> Celebrities often complain that they do not have enough privacy. They say that they are photographed all the time. Pictures are cropped and altered to make them look bad. They don't complain at fees for photos in celebrity magazines. They like their films publicised. They can't have it both ways.

Guided   **2** The extract uses mainly short sentences. Rewrite the extract, using a variety of sentence types.

....

....

....

....

....

....

....

....

Sentence variety 2

Look at the exam-style question below. **You don't need to answer this question**. Instead, think about what you might include in a response, then answer Questions 1 and 2.

Paper ①

5 Write about a time when you, or someone you know, had to deal with conflict. Your response could be real or imagined.

(40 marks)

A student has written their response to the exam-style question.

> Initially, I was really unsure about how to deal with the problem. Naturally, I felt worried that it would become a serious situation. Unfortunately, it was very complicated and people were upset. Frustratingly, I couldn't sort out the problem on my own and had to ask for help. Eventually, though, I managed to make everything better. Thankfully, we are all friends again now.

Guided 1 What type of opener have they used for every sentence? ....

2 Choose three of their sentences and rewrite them using different openers. One has been done for you.

(a) Finding a way to sort out the problem on my own was impossible.

(b) ....

(c) ....

The seven types of sentence openers are:
- A **pronoun** (I, he, she, they)
- An **article** (a, an, the)
- A **preposition** (below, next to, above, behind, between)
- An **–ing word** (or present participle) (thinking, sighing, running, hurrying, crawling)
- An **adjective** (sad, dark, wobbly, slow, quiet, aggressive)
- An **adverb** (nervously, cautiously, sulkily)
- A **conjunction** (if, because, until, although)

Guided 3 Now write a paragraph in response to the above exam-style question. Aim to use:
- at least four different types of sentence opener in your writing
- a different word to start each of your sentences.

....

....

....

....

....

....

....

....

It is easy to accidentally start a lot of sentences with 'The' or 'I', but this can make your writing sound repetitive.

Sentences for different effects

Read the extract and then answer Question 1.

> The rain lashed in through the open window, drenching everything in the room in seconds; arriving to prevent the damage, I saw that I was too late. A disaster!

Guided 1 In the example above, the final sentence is a minor sentence following a multi-clause sentence. What effect is this intended to have on the reader?

....

....

Read the extract below.

> Hurrying to mop up the water, I assessed the full extent of the damage. All the paperwork and books were saturated and no amount of drying them would help, although I tried hard to make it look less of a wreck. Alarmingly, he would be back soon. Between his arrival and my explanations, I needed a miracle to happen.

Guided 2 Reorder the extract to change the emphasis.

....

....

....

....

Guided 3 Explain how the order in which the information is organised affects the sentence's emphasis.

....

....

Look at the exam-style question below. **You don't need to answer this question.** Instead, think about how you might start your response, then answer Question 4.

Paper ②

8 Write a review of the school's recent big fund-raising event which takes place every year. You could write about:
- how well the event was advertised
- if the event raised much money
- how enjoyable the event was

as well as any other ideas you might have.

(40 marks)

> Avoid overloading a sentence with too much information. While sentence variety is important, a sentence with too many subordinate clauses will struggle to keep its meaning.

Guided 4 Write the opening two or three sentences of your own response to Question 8 above. Aim to include a:
- long multi-clause sentence followed by a single-short clause or minor sentence
- sentence structured to give specific emphasis.

....

....

....

Putting it into practice

 1 Answer the exam-style question below. Focus in particular on varying your sentences for effect.

Paper ②

9 Write an article for the school newsletter exploring the idea that students in Years 10 and 11 should do community work at weekends.

You could write about:

- what sort of community work could be carried out by the students
- how this would benefit students and the community
- any disadvantages or problems with the idea (for example, supervising students, impact on their free time)

as well as any other ideas you might have.

(40 marks)

When you tackle any writing question in the exam you should think about sentence variety. Remember to:

- use a range of sentence types
- start your sentences in different ways
- structure your sentences for effect
- avoid overloading individual sentences with too much information.

....

....

....

....

....

....

....

....

....

....

....

....

....

....

....

....

....

....

....

Remember: You have more space than this to answer your question in the exam. Use your own paper to finish your answer to the question above.

Ending a sentence

Failing to use full stops, question marks, exclamation marks and capital letters correctly affects the quality of your writing.

1 Tick the sentences that use capital letters correctly. One has been done for you.

☐   **A**   I saw her pick up the brick. Then she threw it.

☐   **B**   He never saw me watching, Since I was hidden behind the tree.

☐   **C**   'My name is billy,' he said.

☐   **D**   RSPCA stands for the Royal Society for the Prevention of Cruelty to Animals.

✓   **E**   He went that way! Or was it that way?

2 Write in the punctuation you should use to end each sentence.

(a) The bike was rusty and its paint had chipped off ………

(b) What do you mean you couldn't find the monkey ………

(c) I never really liked him ………

(d) Have you never seen a thousand pounds before ………

(e) Stop or you'll crash ………

> Use a full stop at the end of a sentence, an exclamation mark at the end of an exclamation and a question mark at the end of a question. 'That's what he said!', 'That's what he said.' and 'That's what he said?' have quite different meanings.

3 Write a sentence for each type of ending punctuation. The first one has been done for you.

(a) Full stop: The wind blew him over three times before he finally got home.

(b) Question mark: ....

(c) Exclamation mark: ....

4 Look at the sentences below. Tick the two sentences that are punctuated correctly. Cross the one that is not.

A   I knew he would be really good, it was difficult to get him to agree.

B   I knew he would be really good but it was difficult to get him to agree.

C   I knew he would be really good. It was difficult to get him to agree.

> You do not use a comma to join two pieces of information together in a sentence; this is an error known as **comma splicing**. Use a full stop to separate them or a conjunction to join them together. So when you are about to use a comma, check that both parts of the sentence cannot stand alone as separate sentences.

5 Look at this student's writing. Correct all the full stop, question mark and exclamation mark errors you can find.

The Stand Off

I have no intention of giving in this time, he might think he will get away with it, but I am ready for him now. He will ask for money again with the promise of repaying me next week, but he has never repaid any money I have lent him it is time for me to make a stand. How many more times will he ask me. How long before he is able to get control of his finances! I say this all stops now.

Commas

If you are confident with using commas, you will have more control over your writing. This will make your multi-clause sentences and lists more effective, and enable your reader to better understand you.

1   Look at the sentences below. Some have used commas correctly. Some have not. Tick the correct ones and put a cross by the incorrect ones. One has been done for you.

Commas in lists

☐   **A** People can be less lonely if they have friends, family, a good support network and a sense of security.

☒   **B** I am only happy when, I have my books, suntan lotion and bottled water for a day at the beach.

☐   **C** It can be a flat, a studio, a house, a bungalow so long as we can call it home.

Commas in multi-clause sentences with subordinate clauses

☐   **D** Friends are very important even though some can be hard work.

☐   **E** Although we had a great time we never repeated the experience.

☐   **F** Even though some can be hard work, friends can be very important to us.

Commas in multi-clause sentences with relative clauses

☐   **G** The football pitch, although green in places, was very muddy for the players.

☐   **H** Someone who was very important to me, emigrated to Australia.

☐   **I** The visit, which we only made once was a huge success.

Look at the exam-style question below. **You don't need to answer this question**. Instead, think about what you might include in a response, then answer Question 2.

Paper ①

5   Write about a time when you, or someone you know, made a lasting impression. Your response could be real or imagined.

(40 marks)

Gui̶ded

2   Write three sentences in response to the exam-style question above. Use commas differently each time.

(a)   Items in a list

....

....

(b)   A main and a subordinate clause

....

....

(c)   A main and relative clause

....

....

Apostrophes and speech punctuation

Make sure you know how to avoid common errors in using apostrophes and speech punctuation.

1 Look at the sentences below. Some have used apostrophes correctly. Some have not. Tick the correct ones and cross the incorrect ones. One has been done for you.

Apostrophes in contractions

☐ **A** I'm so pleased with my test results.

☐ **B** Its not my homework.

☐ **C** She hasnt finished her homework.

> **Remember:** **it's** always means 'it is'. **Its** means 'something belonging to it'.

Apostrophes of possession

☑ **D** My sister's bag broke.

☐ **E** The girls' costumes were superb.

☐ **F** The tutor groups project was a charity talent show.

Speech punctuation

☐ **G** 'Look out'! he yelled.

☐ **H** 'Don't worry,' she said.

☐ **I** 'You need to stop doing that.' he instructed.

> Often, instead of the double inverted commas for speech: " ", we use the single ' '. This is the same symbol that we use for an apostrophe.

Guided 2 Look again at all the sentences in Question 1. Correct any you marked as incorrect.

3 Now read this conversation between two friends in which they discuss the behaviour of a new student. Add in the missing apostrophes and speech marks and then write the rest of the conversation.

Hey, she called. You'll never guess what happened in History today. ....

Whats that? I asked. I didn't go because my dads car broke down. Its engine wouldnt start ...

Billy dropped Staceys pencil case into Misss fish tank. It landed on top of the fishs castle. I

dont know if its still in there because Im too scared to check ....

Was Miss mad? I asked. I wouldve been and I heard shes well scary when shes mad ....

She was really scary. Werent you there when ....

....

....

....

....

....

....

> **Remember:**
> • apostrophes in contractions are used to replace missing letters
> • apostrophes of possession are always placed at the end of the noun, whether it's plural (teachers') or singular (teacher's)
> • in dialogue, there is always a punctuation mark before the closing speech marks.

Colons, semi-colons, dashes, brackets and ellipses

Punctuation helps you to express yourself clearly, develop your ideas and gain control over your writing.

1 Draw lines to match the names of the types of punctuation with the correct symbols and statements.

Dashes	( )	This suggests missing information or a dramatic pause.
Ellipses	;	You can use this to link two connected ideas.
Brackets	…	These are used in pairs to add extra information.
Semi-colons	:	This can be used singularly or in pairs to add extra information to a sentence.
Colons	- *or* —	This introduces an example, list or explanation.

2 Look at the sentences below. In each of them an ellipsis, a semicolon, a colon or a dash has been used incorrectly, or could be replaced by other punctuation instead. Correct the sentences.

A To everyone's surprise; the magician had completely vanished…

To everyone's surprise, the magician had completely vanished.

B A healthy diet is vital … it can allow you to gain an edge over competitors – who don't take care of their bodies.

....

C Learning to be a good loser is: essential. Everybody tastes defeat at some point.

....

D (I have always been good at the flute) … since I can remember anyway but wanted to be better.

....

E Some cyclists take to the road; without wearing a safety helmet … not a good idea.

....

Look at the exam-style question below. **You don't need to answer this question**. Instead, think about what you might include in a response, then answer Question 3.

Paper ①

5 Write about a time when you, or someone you know, helped a person or an animal in difficulty. Your response could be real or imagined. **(40 marks)**

3 Write three to five sentences in response to the exam-style question above. Try to use:

- a colon and semi-colon
- dashes, brackets and an ellipsis.

....

....

....

....

....

Putting it into practice

 1 Answer the exam-style question below. Focus in particular on punctuation.

Paper ②

8 Write a letter to the 'Community Action Group', applying for voluntary work in the summer holidays.

In your letter you could:
- explain why you are interested in working with the action group
- describe the areas where you think you have particular strengths and interests
- explain why you would be a useful addition to the action group team

as well as any other ideas you might have.

(40 marks)

When you tackle any writing in the exam, you should think of punctuation. Remember to:
- use a range of punctuation accurately, including advanced punctuation, such as colons and semi-colons
- plan your time carefully, so that you have time to check the accuracy of your punctuation.

....
....
....
....
....
....
....
....
....
....
....
....
....
....
....
....
....
....
....
....

Remember: You have more space than this to answer your question in the exam. Use your own paper to finish your answer to the question above.

Common spelling errors 1

Some of the most common spelling errors in students' writing are a result of misusing or confusing the following:

would of and would have should of and should have could of and could have	'have' is correct; this mistake occurs because people say 'would've', omitting the 'have', which makes it sound like 'would of'
our and are	our – belongs to us, e.g. 'That's our house.' are – auxiliary verb used to form plural present progressive tense, e.g. 'we are looking', a continuous present action
their, there and they're	their – belongs to them there – over there, position they're – they are
affect and effect	'affect' is usually a verb, meaning to make a difference to 'effect' is usually a noun, meaning the result of something One way can be to think of **A**ffect being a c**A**use, and **E**ffect being a r**E**sult.
Words ending in -ley and -le	The most common ending is -ly. It's used when creating an adverb. terrible – terribly slow – slowly beautiful – beautifully
its and it's	'it's' always means 'it is' 'its' means 'belonging to it'

 Guided

1 Using the information above to help you, choose the correct spellings to complete the sentences below.

(a) .... books were soaked and covered in wet grass.
     Their   There   They're

(b) The dog lifted .... injured paw.
     its   it's

(c) We are all .... by people's moods.
     affected   effected

(d) The abandoned shed is over ....
     their   there   they're

(e) We .... finished that if we hadn't given up.
     could have   could of

(f) .... you ready yet? We don't want to miss the bus.
     Are   Our

(g) When people are cheerful, we respond ....
     positively   positivley

(h) You .... thought of that before we left the house.
     should have   should of

> • There are very few words ending in ley.
> • **Would of, could of** and **should of** are **always** incorrect.

Common spelling errors 2

Some of the most common spelling errors in students' writing are a result of misusing or confusing the following:

your and *you're*	Your – a pronoun, used to address someone directly You're – means 'you are'
two, too and *to*	two – the number, e.g. 'two things you need' too – also or excessively, e.g. 'she saw things too', 'that was too much' to – preposition showing relationship of time or place, e.g. 'I went to the park', 'It is going to rain'
we're, *were*, *where* and *wear*	we're – 'we are' were – past tense; 'we were singing' where – shows location wear – 'I wear a coat'
of and *off*	off – usually shows disconnection; opposite of on, e.g. 'I ran off', 'turn off' of – a preposition, usually shows connection, e.g. 'the brother of', 'a part of'
whose and *who's*	whose – shows belonging, e.g. 'whose pyjamas are these?' who's – means 'who is'
passed and *past*	passed – verb form, a variation of 'to pass', e.g. 'I passed him on the street' past – never a verb, but flexible; often used to describe history, 'In the past' or as a preposition 'I drove past the gate' (drove is the verb, past describes the distance)

> **Remember:**
> • **A lot** is two words. '**Alot** of people make this mistake' is wrong but '**A lot** of people make this mistake' is correct.
> • For there and their and were and where think: '**Where** is the book, **there** it is, it is **here**.' Also: 'There is **their** son, he is **heir** to **their** business empire.'

1 Correct the spelling errors in bold in these sentences. One has been done for you.

(a) We should go out today: **you're** sister can come too.   *your*

(b) They **where** so lucky that the weather was good for the race. ....

(c) I enjoy learning about **passed** events in history. ....

(d) I thought there were three bottles of water, but there are only **too**. ....

(e) You obviously got caught in the rain as **your** soaked! ....

⟩Guided⟩ **2** Identify and correct the spelling errors in these sentences.

(a) He climbed to the top off the hill. ....

(b) We need to clear the room. Who's jacket is on the chair? ....

(c) The weather is so unpredictable; it is hard to decide what to were. ....

(d) She was so pleased when she past her exams with good grades. ....

(e) He wanted too go to the beach but everyone thought it was too cold. ....

Common spelling errors 3

Twenty-one of the most frequently misspelt words are jumbled with incorrect versions below.

(argument)

dissappoint

occasionally

diffacult

begining

difficult

ocasionally

~~arguement~~

conshence

separately

conscience

weird

independence

consious

embarrassing

possession

business

experiance

rythm

buisness

seperately

embarassing

independance

rhythm

conscious

experience

reccomend

recommend

definately

greatful

desicion

decision

disappear

posession

believe

grateful

disapear

definitely

disappoint

beginning

beleive

wierd

> Correct spelling **can be learned**. Every time you spell a word incorrectly, make a note of the word and start to practise the correct spelling on a regular basis. Try strategies like looking for a hidden word within the word you are learning to spell, or saying what you see.

---

1 Find the word pairs above. In each pair, there is one correct spelling and one incorrect spelling. Circle the correct spelling and cross out the incorrect spelling.

2 Now check your answers. For any of the spellings causing you difficulty, make up a sentence with a tip for remembering the word. An example has been done for you:

I can recommend two 'm's in recommend. ....

....

....

....

....

....

....

....

....

Proofreading

Proofreading is important so that you can correct any errors before you hand in your paper at the end of the exam. Plan your time so that you are able to check your work carefully and fix any mistakes.

1 Look at the extract from one student's writing below. Read it carefully, looking for any:

- spelling errors
- punctuation errors
- grammatical errors (e.g. misused, repeated or missing words).

Circle or underline the errors and correct them. One has been done for you.

> _were_
> As usual, we (where) waiting for the bus by the entrance too the national park. It was some time before we realised what was going on. Their was the noise of something crashing about in the undergrowth and then little cries of distress. We are not the bravest people in the world, but the buss was'nt due for ages and there wear others out and about if we needed help.
>
> Advancing cautiously, we crept into the undergrowth and their trapped in the branches of a low-hanging tree, was a very young beautiful baby deer. It wasn't afrade of us; it kept still as we fredd it then it scampered away no harm done!

 2 Look back at three or four pieces of writing you have completed recently. How many errors can you find? In the table below, note down the correct way to spell the words you have misspelt and the kinds of punctuation and grammatical errors you have made.

> Try to 'take a step back' from your writing and imagine you are checking someone else's work. Whenever you think you are likely to make an error, stop and check your work. This is a good preparation for writing under time pressure in the exam.

Spelling errors	Punctuation errors	Grammatical errors

 3 Using your answers to Question 2, practise looking for errors by proofreading the answers you have written in this workbook. Fix any mistakes you find.

Putting it into practice

 1 Answer the exam-style question below. Focus in particular on proofreading your answer.

 9 Write an article for the school magazine in which you explore a proposal by the school to extend the school day and have Saturday classes for GCSE students.
You could write about:
- the plan for the students in detail
- your views on each part of the proposal
- how these changes might benefit or disadvantage the students

as well as any other ideas you might have.   **(40 marks)**

When you tackle any writing question in the exam, remember to:
- allow time after you have finished writing to check the accuracy of your work
- look out for the spelling, punctuation and grammatical errors that you know you tend to make so that you can correct them.

....
....
....
....
....
....
....
....
....
....
....
....
....
....
....
....
....
....
....
....
....

Remember: You have more space than this to answer your question in the exam. Use your own paper to finish your answer to the question above.

Cut along the dotted lines and staple the texts together to make your own handy anthology. Make sure you keep it safe with your Workbook.

Text 1

This is an extract from a novel. Here, the narrator called Pip has returned from a visit to the mysterious Miss Havisham and his sister and Mr Pumblechook want to know all the details

Great Expectations: Charles Dickens

'Boy! What like is Miss Havisham?' Mr Pumblechook began again when he had recovered; folding his arms tight on his chest and applying the screw.

'Very tall and dark,' I told him.

'Is she, uncle?' asked my sister.

Mr Pumblechook winked assent; from which I inferred that he had never seen Miss Havisham, for she was nothing of the kind.   5

'Good!' said Mr Pumblechook, conceitedly. ('This is the way to have him! We are beginning to hold our own, I think, Mum?')

'I am sure, uncle,' returned Mrs Joe, 'I wish you had him always: you know so well how to deal with him.'

'Now, boy! What was she a doing of, when you went in today?' asked Mr Pumblechook.   10

'She was sitting,' I answered, 'in a black velvet coach.'

Mr Pumblechook and Mrs Joe stared at one another – as well they might – and both repeated, 'In a black velvet coach?'

'Yes,' said I. 'And Miss Estella – that's her niece, I think – handed her in cake and wine at the coach window, on a gold plate. And we all had cake and wine on gold plates. And I got up behind the   15
coach to eat mine, because she told me to.'

'Was anyone else there?' asked Mr Pumblechook.

'Four dogs,' said I.

'Large or small?'

'Immense,' said I. 'And they fought for veal cutlets[1] out of a silver basket.'   20

Mr Pumblechook and Mrs Joe stared at one another again in utter amazement. I was perfectly frantic – a reckless witness under the torture – and would have told them anything.

'Where *was* this coach, in the name of gracious?' asked my sister.

'In Miss Havisham's room.' They stared again. 'But there weren't any horses to it.' I added this saving clause, in the moment of rejecting four richly caparisoned coursers[2], which I had had wild   25
thoughts of harnessing.

'Can this be possible, uncle?' asked Mrs Joe. 'What can the boy mean?'

'I'll tell you, Mum,' said Mr Pumblechook. 'My opinion is, it's a sedan chair[3]. She's flighty, you know – very flighty – quite flighty enough to pass her days in a sedan chair.'

'Did you ever see her in it, uncle?' asked Mrs Joe.   30

'How could I,' he returned, forced to the admission, 'when I never see her in my life? Never clapped eyes upon her!'

'Goodness, uncle! And yet you have spoken to her?'

'Why, don't you know,' said Mr Pumblechook testily, 'that when I have been there, I have been took up to the outside of her door, and the door has been stood ajar, and she has spoke to me that way.   35
Don't say you don't know *that*, Mum. Howsever, the boy went there to play. What did you play at, boy?'

'We played with flags,' I said. (I beg to observe that I think of myself with amazement, when I recall the lies I told on this occasion.)

'Flags!' echoed my sister.

'Yes,' said I. 'Estella waved a blue flag and I waved a red one, and Miss Havisham waved one   40
sprinkled all over with little gold stars, out of the coach window. And then we all waved our swords and hurrahed.'

'Swords!' repeated my sister. 'Where did you get swords from?'

'Out of a cupboard,' said I. 'And I saw pistols in it – and jam – and pills. And there was no daylight in the room, but it was all lighted up with candles.'   45

'That's true, Mum,' said Mr Pumblechook, with a grave nod. 'That's the state of the case, for that much I've seen myself.' And then they both stared at me, and I, with an obtrusive[4] show of artlessness[5] on my countenance[6], stared at them, and plaited[7] the right leg of my trousers with my right hand.

If they had asked me any more questions I should undoubtedly have betrayed myself, for I was even then on the point of mentioning that there was a balloon in the yard, and should have hazarded[8] the   50
statement but for my invention being divided between that phenomenon and a bear in the brewery[9]. They were so much occupied, however, in discussing the marvels I had already presented for their consideration, that I escaped.

1: *veal cutlets* – thin slices of calf meat

2: *caparisoned coursers* – large powerful horses dressed in decorated cloth coverings

3: *sedan chair* – an enclosed chair carried on poles by two people

4: *obtrusive* – noticeable

5: *artlessness* – lack of deception

6: *countenance* – facial expression

7: *plaited* – pleated or folded over

8: *hazarded* – guessed without confidence

9: *brewery* – a place where beer is made

Cut along the dotted lines and staple the texts together to make your own handy anthology. Make sure you keep it safe with your Workbook.

TEXTS

Text 2

> This is an extract from a novel. Mary and Rosamond are friends who are disagreeing about Fred, Rosamond's brother.

Middlemarch: George Eliot

'Haughtiness[1] is not conceit[2]; I call Fred conceited.'

'I wish no one said any worse of him. He should be more careful. Mrs Waule has been telling uncle that Fred is very unsteady.' Mary spoke from a girlish impulse which got the better of her judgement. There was a vague uneasiness associated with the word 'unsteady' which she hoped Rosamond might say something to dissipate[3]. But she purposely abstained[4] from mentioning Mrs Waule's more special insinuation[5].   5

'Oh, Fred is horrid!' said Rosamond. She would not have allowed herself so unsuitable a word to anyone but Mary.

'What do you mean by horrid?'

'He is so idle, and makes Papa so angry, and says he will not take orders[6].'   10

'I think Fred is quite right.'

'How can you say he is right, Mary? I thought you had more sense of religion.'

'He is not fit to be a clergyman[7].'

'But he ought to be fit.'

'Well, then, he is not what he ought to be. I know some other people who are in the same case.'   15

'But no one approves of them. I should not like to marry a clergyman; but there must be clergymen.'

'It does not follow that Fred must be one.'

'But when Papa has been at the expense of educating him for it! And only suppose, if he should have no fortune left him?'

'I can suppose that very well,' said Mary, dryly.   20

'Then I wonder you can defend Fred,' said Rosamond, inclined to push this point.

'I don't defend him,' said Mary laughing; 'I would defend any parish from having him for a clergyman.'

'But of course if he were a clergyman, he must be different.'

'Yes, he would be a great hypocrite[8]; and he is not that yet.'

'It is no use saying anything to you, Mary. You always take Fred's part.'   25

'Why should I not take his part?' said Mary, lighting up. 'He would take mine. He is the only person who takes the least trouble to oblige[9] me.'

'You make me feel very uncomfortable, Mary,' said Rosamond, with her gravest mildness;

'I would not tell Mamma for the world.'

'What would you not tell her?' said Mary, angrily.   30

'Pray, do not go into a rage, Mary,' sad Rosamond, mildly as ever.

'If your mamma is afraid that Fred will make me an offer, tell her that I would not marry him if he asked me. But he is not going to do so, that I am aware. He certainly has never asked me.'

'Mary, you are always so violent.'

'And you are always so exasperating.'   35

'I? What can you blame me for?'

'Oh, blameless people are always the most exasperating. There is the bell – I think we must go down.'

'I did not mean to quarrel,' said Rosamond, putting on her hat.

'Quarrel? Nonsense; we have not quarrelled. If one is not to get into a rage sometimes, what is the good of being friends?'   40

'Am I to repeat what you have said?'

'Just as you please. I never say what I am afraid of having repeated. But let us go down.'

1: *haughtiness* – appearing proud or arrogant
2: *conceit* – being proud or vain
3: *dissipate* – make something disappear
4: *abstained* – stopped herself
5: *insinuation* – hint of something unpleasant

6: *orders* – a religious ceremony to become a clergyman
7: *clergyman* – a male member of the church
8: *hypocrite* – someone who goes against their beliefs
9: *oblige* – do as someone asks

TEXTS

Cut along the dotted lines and staple the texts together to make your own
handy anthology. Make sure you keep it safe with your Workbook.

Text 3

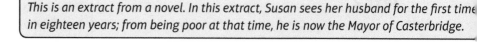

This is an extract from a novel. In this extract, Susan sees her husband for the first time in eighteen years; from being poor at that time, he is now the Mayor of Casterbridge.

The Mayor of Casterbridge: Thomas Hardy

Facing the window, in the chair of dignity, sat a man about forty years of age; of heavy frame, large features, and commanding voice; his general build being rather coarse than compact. He had a rich complexion, which verged on swarthiness[1], a flashing black eye, and dark, bushy brows and hair.

When he indulged in an occasional loud laugh at some remark among the guests, his large mouth parted so far back as to show the rays of the chandelier a full score or more of the two-and-thirty sound white teeth that he could obviously still boast of. 5

That laugh was not encouraging to strangers; and hence it may have been well that it was rarely heard. Many theories have been built upon it. It fell in well with conjectures[2] of a temperament which would have no pity for weakness, but it would be ready to yield ungrudging admiration to greatness and strength. Its producer's personal goodness, if he had any, would be of a very fitful cast – an occasional almost oppressive generosity rather than a mild and constant kindness. 10

Susan Henchard's husband – in law, at least – sat before them, matured in shape, stiffened in line, exaggerated in traits, disciplined, thought-marked – in a word, older. Elizabeth, encumbered with no recollections as her mother was, regarded him with nothing more than the keen curiosity and interest which the discovery of such unexpected social standing in the long-sought relative naturally begot. He was dressed in an old-fashioned evening suit, an expanse of frilled shirt showing on his broad breast, jewelled studs, and a heavy gold chain. Three glasses stood at his right hand; but, to his wife's surprise, the two for wine were empty, while the third, a tumbler, was half full of water. 15

When last she had seen him he was sitting in a corduroy[3] jacket, fustian[4] waistcoat and breeches, and tanned leather leggings, with a basin of hot furmity[5] before him. Time, the magician, had wrought much here. Watching him, and thus thinking of past days, she became so moved that she shrank back against the jamb[6] of the waggon-office doorway to which the steps gave access, the shadow from it conveniently hiding her features. She forgot her daughter till a touch from Elizabeth-Jane aroused her. 'Have you seen him, mother?' whispered the girl. 20

'Yes, yes,' answered her companion hastily. 'I have seen him, and it is enough for me! Now I want to go – pass away – die.' 25

'Why – Oh what?' She drew closer, and whispered in her mother's ear, 'Does he seem to you not likely to befriend us? I thought he looked a generous man. What a gentleman he is, isn't he? And how his diamond studs shine! How strange that you should have said he might be in the stocks, or in the workhouse, or dead! Did ever anything go more by contraries! Why should you feel so afraid of him? I am not at all; I'll call upon him – he can but say he don't own such remote kin.' 30

1: *swarthiness* – a dark complexion
2: *conjectures* – an opinion without all the information
3: *corduroy* – a fabric made up of a cord pattern
4: *fustian* – heavily woven, coarse cotton cloth
5: *furmity* – dish of wheat boiled in milk with cinnamon
6: *jamb* – post or side of a doorway

Cut along the dotted lines and staple the texts together to make your own handy anthology. Make sure you keep it safe with your Workbook.

TEXTS

Text 4

> *This is an extract from a novel. Housekeeper Miss Dean is telling her guest about the time when Heathcliff, a child, is rescued from the streets by Mr Earnshaw and how this affects the whole family, including Hindley, Mr Earnshaw's son.*

Wuthering Heights: Emily Brontë

So, from the very beginning, he bred bad feeling in the house; and at Mrs Earnshaw's death, which happened in less than two years after, the young master had learnt to regard his father as an oppressor rather than a friend, and Heathcliff as a usurper of his father's affections, and his privileges, and he grew bitter with brooding over these injuries. I sympathised awhile, but, when the children fell ill of the measles and I had to tend them, and take on me the cares of a woman at once, I changed my ideas. Heathcliff was dangerously sick; and while he lay at the worst he would have me constantly by his pillow; I suppose he felt I did a good deal for him, and he hadn't wit to guess that I was compelled to do it. However, I will say this, he was the quietest child that ever a nurse watched over. The difference between him and the others forced me to be less partial. Cathy and her brother harassed me terribly: he was as uncomplaining as a lamb; though hardness, not gentleness, made him give little trouble. 5, 10

He got through, and the doctor affirmed it was in a great measure owing to me, and praised me for my care. I was vain of his commendations, and softened towards the being by whose means I earned them, and thus Hindley lost his last ally; still I couldn't dote[1] on Heathcliff, and I wondered often what my master saw to admire so much in the sullen boy who never, to my recollection, repaid his indulgence by any sign of gratitude. He was not insolent[2] to his benefactor[3], he was simply insensible; though knowing perfectly the hold he had on his heart, and conscious he had only to speak and all the house obliged to bend to his wishes. 15

As an instance, I remember Mr Earnshaw bought a couple of colts at the parish fair, and gave the lads each one. Heathcliff took the handsomest, but it soon fell lame, and when he discovered it, he said to Hindley, 20

'You must exchange horses with me; I don't like mine, and if you won't I shall tell your father of the three lashings[4] you've given me this week, and show him my arm, which is black to the shoulder.' Hindley put out his tongue and cuffed him over the ears.

'You'd better do it at once,' he persisted, escaping to the porch (they were in the stable): 'you will have to; and if I speak of these blows, you'll get them again with interest.' 25

'Off dog!' cried Hindley, threatening him with an iron weight, used for weighing potatoes and hay.

'Throw it,' he replied, standing still, 'and then I'll tell how you boasted that you would turn me out of doors as soon as he died, and see whether he will not turn you out directly.'

Hindley threw it, hitting him on the breast, and down he fell, but staggered up immediately, breathless and white; and, had I not prevented it, he would have gone just so to the master, and got full revenge by letting his condition plead for him, intimating who had caused it. 30

1: *dote* – fuss about and be fond of
2: *insolent* – disrespectful
3: *benefactor* – someone who gives money
4: *lashings* – beatings

Cut along the dotted lines and staple the texts together to make your own handy anthology. Make sure you keep it safe with your Workbook.

Text 5

Emmeline Pankhurst was one of the leaders of the women's movement in early 20th-century Britain to obtain the right to vote. This is an extract from a speech she delivered in Hartford, Connecticut in America on 13 November 1913.

Freedom or death

Your forefathers decided that they must have representation for taxation, many, many years ago. When they felt they couldn't wait any longer, when they laid all the arguments before an obstinate British government that they could think of, and when their arguments were absolutely disregarded, when every other means had failed, they began by the tea party at Boston, and they went on until they had won the independence of the United States of America. 5

It is about eight years since the word militant[1] was first used to describe what we were doing. It was not militant at all, except that it provoked militancy on the part of those who were opposed to it. When women asked questions in political meetings and failed to get answers, they were not doing anything militant. In Great Britain it is a custom, a time-honoured one, to ask questions of candidates for parliament and ask questions of members of the government. No man was ever 10 put out of a public meeting for asking a question. The first people who were put out of a political meeting for asking questions were women; they were brutally ill-used; they found themselves in jail before 24 hours had expired.

We were called militant, and we were quite willing to accept the name. We were determined to press this question of the enfranchisement[2] of women to the point where we were no longer to be ignored 15 by the politicians.

You have two babies very hungry and wanting to be fed. One baby is a patient baby, and waits indefinitely until its mother is ready to feed it. The other baby is an impatient baby and cries lustily, screams and kicks and makes everybody unpleasant until it is fed. Well, we know perfectly well which baby is attended to first. That is the whole history of politics. You have to make more noise 20 than anybody else, you have to make yourself more obtrusive[3] than anybody else, you have to fill all the papers more than anybody else, in fact you have to be there all the time and see that they do not snow you under.

When you have warfare things happen; people suffer; the non-combatants suffer as well as the combatants. And so it happens in civil war. When your forefathers threw the tea into Boston 25 Harbour, a good many women had to go without their tea. It has always seemed to me an extraordinary thing that you did not follow it up by throwing the whiskey overboard; you sacrificed the women; and there is a good deal of warfare for which men take a great deal of glorification which has involved more practical sacrifice on women than it has on any man. It always has been so. The grievances of those who have got power, the influence of those who have got power 30 commands a great deal of attention; but the wrongs and the grievances of those people who have no power at all are apt to be absolutely ignored. That is the history of humanity right from the beginning.

Well, in our civil war people have suffered, but you cannot make omelettes without breaking eggs; you cannot have civil war without damage to something. The great thing is to see that no more damage is done than is absolutely necessary, that you do just as much as will arouse enough feeling 35 to bring about peace, to bring about an honourable peace for the combatants; and that is what we have been doing.

1: *militant* – someone using conflict or violence to achieve a cause
2: *enfranchisement* – the right to vote
3: *obtrusive* – noticeable

Cut along the dotted lines and staple the texts together to make your own handy anthology. Make sure you keep it safe with your Workbook.

TEXTS

Text 6

This is an extract from an online article by Cecile Borkhataria for DailyMail.com about the use of fidget spinners.

Are fidget spinners a scam? Researchers say there is no proof the hit toys help people with ADHD and autism

- Fidget spinners are small devices that a person can spin between his/her fingers
- They're being sold everywhere from internet retailer to street vendor and stores
- The device has even been marketed as an aid for ADHD, autism and anxiety, however no formal academic studies on their effect have been conducted
- In response to the emergence of the new toy, some schools have banned them from being used in classrooms, claiming they're distracting students

Before December 2016, a Google Trends search revealed that searches for the term fidget spinner were low, but increased rapidly in the New Year.

There are thousands of YouTube videos about how to spin the device and use tricks, and there's even a subreddit page dedicated solely to fidget spinners.

Different designs of the device vary in cost between $1 for standard spinners, to $59.99 for top of the range versions, such as Stealth Fidget Spinners' Aventador Fidget Spinner which can spin for a period of four to seven minutes.

The devices are also regularly marketed for helping to provide increased focus and stress relief for people who have Attention Deficit Disorder (ADD), Attention Deficit Hyperactivity Disorder (ADHD), Anxiety and Autism – however, there is no proof to support this claim.

Dr Mark Rapport, MD and Director of the Children's Learning Clinic at the University of Central Florida's Department of Psychology, told the DailyMail.com that while his current and past research indicates that many children with ADHD benefit from some forms of movement when engaged in challenging cognitive tasks, he has not come across any studies examining the potential benefits or adverse effects of fidget spinners.

Dr Rapport's 2015 study found that children with ADHD who participated in activities involving 'gross body movement', which is movement of the limbs or large parts of the body, performed better than those who sat still during memory tasks.

However, fidget spinners don't require the user to engage in gross body movement, which appears to increase brain arousal necessary to engage in many cognitive tasks, said Dr Rapport. 'Using a spinner like gadget is more likely to serve as a distraction than a benefit for individuals with ADHD,' he said.

This is because the gadget requires some level of attention to operate, which diverts the users attention away from what they should be viewing.

'Riding a stationary bike while reading or sitting on a movement ball while working at one's desk, in contrast, allows small (non-distracting) motor movements and would probably prove beneficial for many children with ADHD,' said Dr Rapport.

The devices may not just be distracting to users – they're also proving to be a nuisance to teachers. Gerrell Knighsthead, an elementary school PE teacher in Paso Robles, California, posted a picture of fidget spinners on Twitter, writing: 'If another one of my students brings one of these to class I'm gonna lose my mind #teacherstruggles #fidgetspinner.'

In response to the emergence of the new toy, some schools have banned them from being used in classrooms. Kate Ellison, principal of Washington Elementary School in Evanston, Illinois, where the toys have been banned, told the *Chicago Tribune*: 'Frankly, we've found the fidgets (spinners) were having the opposite effect of what they advertise.

'Kids are trading them or spinning them instead of writing.'

However, some parents who have children with mental health disorders have praised the device.

Miriam Gwynne, a mother of an 8-year-old daughter with autism, wrote on autismawareness.com that the device has made her daughter less stressed and self-conscious about her need to fidget at school.

'Mum, it's like everyone wants to be autistic like me now!' Gwynne's daughter told her.

Despite different claims, the only way to truly determine the effect of fidget spinners is to conduct a study on them.

But Dr Rapport told the DailyMail.com that it's 'highly unlikely' that his team will.

'It requires considerable time and resources to conduct a well-controlled clinical study and the businesses that produce these devices would need to foot the bill ... moreover, if the results were negative they would have to temper their exaggerated claims,' he said.

TEXTS

Cut along the dotted lines and staple the texts together to make your own handy anthology. Make sure you keep it safe with your Workbook.

Text 7

This is an extract from a travel book in which Bill Bryson, visiting from the US, describes his arrival in Bournemouth in the 1990s.

Notes from a Small Island: Bill Bryson

And so to Bournemouth. I arrived at five-thirty in the evening in a driving rain. Night had fallen heavily and the streets were full of swishing cars, their headlights sweeping through bullets of shiny rain. I'd lived in Bournemouth for two years and thought I knew it reasonably well, but the area around the station had been extensively rebuilt, with new roads and office blocks and one of those befuddling networks of pedestrian subways that compel you to surface every few minutes like a gopher to see where you are.   5

By the time I reached the East Cliff, a neighbourhood of medium-sized hotels perched high above a black sea, I was soaked through and muttering. The only thing to be said for Bournemouth is that you are certainly spoiled for choice with hotels. Among the many gleaming palaces of comfort that lined every street for blocks around, I selected an establishment on a side-street for no good reason   10
other than that I rather liked its sign: neat capitals in pink neon glowing beckoningly through the slicing rain. I stepped inside, shedding water and could see at a glance it was a good choice – clean, nicely old-fashioned, attractively priced at £26 B&B according to a notice on the wall, and with the kind of smothering warmth that makes your glasses steam and brings on sneezing fits. I decanted several ounces of water from my sleeve and asked for a single room for two nights.   15

'Is it raining out?' the reception girl asked brightly as I filled in the registration card between the sneezes and pauses to wipe wet water from my face with the back of my arm.

'No, my ship sank and I had to swim the last seven miles.'

'Oh yes?' she went on in a manner that made me suspect she was not attending my words closely.

'And will you be dining with us tonight, Mr – ' she glanced at my water-smeared card ' – Mr   20
Brylcreem?' I considered the alternative – a long slog through stair-rods of rain – and felt inclined to stay in. Besides, between her cheerily bean-sized brain and my smeared scrawl, there was every chance they would charge the meal to another room. I said I'd eat in, accepted a key and drippingly found my way to my room.

Among the many hundreds of things that have come a long way in Britain since 1973, and if you   25
stop to think about it even for a moment you'll see that the list is impressively long, few have come further than the average English hostelry. Nowadays you get a colour TV, coffee-making tray with a little packet of modestly tasty biscuits, a private bath with fluffy towels, a little basket of cotton wool in rainbow colours, and an array of sachets or little plastic bottles of shampoo, bath gel and moisturizing lotion. My room even had an adequate bedside light and two soft pillows. I was very happy.   30

Cut along the dotted lines and staple the texts together to make your own handy anthology. Make sure you keep it safe with your Workbook.

TEXTS

Text 8

This is an article about 'Letter to a Teen-ager' by Doris S. Burville.

Guidance from the Past

I'm sure you've heard that common complaint of teenagers all over the world: 'That's boring', 'This is boring' or simply 'I'm bored'. But is it a new problem? The answer is no, and the solution isn't new either. A Letter to the Editor from 1955 has been unearthed that tells the teenagers of the time to grow up and entertain themselves, which many argue rings true to our adolescents today. In fact, it's been shared, retweeted and quoted so many times that it's at risk of going viral: 5

Letter to a Teenager

Doris S. Burville

'Always we hear the plaintive cry of the teenager, 'What can we do? Where can we go?' The answer is, go home!

'Hang the storm windows, paint the woodwork. Rake the leaves, mow the lawn, shovel the walk. Wash the car, learn to cook, scrub some floors. Repair the sink, build a boat, get a job.   10

'Help the minister, priest or rabbi, the Red Cross, the Salvation Army. Visit the sick, assist the poor, study your lessons.

'And then when you are through — and not too tired — read a book.

'Your parents do not owe you entertainment. Your city or village does not owe you recreational facilities. The world does not owe you a living. You owe the world something. You owe it your time and energy and your talents so that no one will be at war or in poverty or sick or lonely again.   15

'In plain, simple words, GROW UP; quit being a crybaby. Get out of your dream world and develop a backbone, not a wishbone, and start acting like an adult.

'You're supposed to be mature enough to accept some of the responsibility your parents have carried for years. They have nursed, protected, helped, appealed, begged, excused, tolerated and denied themselves needed comforts so that you could have every benefit. This they have done gladly, for you are their dearest treasure. But now, you have no right to expect them to bow to every whim and fancy just because selfish ego, instead of common sense, dominates your personality, thinking and requests.   20

'In heaven's name, grow up and go home!'

Opinions are divided on this old-school advice. Is it too harsh, or is it an honest truth that needs to be said? Some argue that it is the parents' responsibility to entertain their children until they are old enough to leave the home, while those on the other side of the fence suggest it is ridiculous for teenagers to expect to be pandered to. Not many 18 year olds would be thrilled if their parents accompanied them out with their friends (unless the parents were paying), so surely that means they forfeit the right to moan when left to their own devices.   25   30

Or perhaps it doesn't even matter, as Peter Scott tweeted on 4 January 2018:

'Be bored or don't be: just stop complaining about it!'

AMENDMENT (16 April 2018): This article wrongly dated the 'Be bored…' quote to 4 January 2018, but it has since been confirmed as 12 December 2017.

Cut along the dotted lines and staple the texts together to make your own handy anthology. Make sure you keep it safe with your Workbook.

Text 9

This article was written by Cara Byington, Science Communication Specialist for the Nature Conservancy.

Wayward plastic is becoming a problem for marine mammals and sea turtles in The Bahamas

'Plastics aren't the only problem, just one of the most obvious. All over the world, animals are dying from eating our trash.'
– Cara Byington

5 I did it again today; I forgot to bring my reusable shopping bags to the grocery store. Actually, I'm a little embarrassed that I didn't even think of them until my son gasped in horror and said, under his breath, 'Mom, she's putting our groceries in plastic!'
10 Crisis.
My first thought is that I have two antsy kids with me who have their hearts set on eating today – but a second later, I find myself thinking about that dead sperm whale I saw on Warderick Wells Cay in The
15 Bahamas.
The connection between the two? The plastic bags.

Plastics: 1, Marine Mammals: 0

Plastic bags, plastic cups, plastic sheeting, plastic bottles, plastic toys, plastic, plastic, plastic. There's even a patch of Pacific Ocean – thought to be at
20 least the size of Texas and dubbed the Great Pacific Garbage Patch – comprised of plastic and other trash, bobbing along at the surface, circling in the current.
But plastics aren't the only problem, just one of the
25 most obvious. All over the world, animals, especially marine mammals and sea turtles, are dying from eating our trash.
In August of 2014, a young female sei whale, which is an endangered species, was found dead in the
30 Chesapeake Bay. A broken DVD case was identified as the cause of death.
That same year, scientists reviewed seabird necropsies (an autopsy of an animal) and found that 90% of seabirds found dead on the beach have
35 ingested plastic.
In 2013, a sperm whale washed up on Spain's southern coast. Its stomach contents? An astonishing 17kg of plastic including clothing hangers, ice cream containers, and plastic sheeting.
40 Of course, reading about sperm whales dying by eating plastic bags they mistake for squid is one thing. Standing behind the long, white ribs of a once-living whale that died by eating plastic is something else entirely.

Skeleton on the Beach

45 Every time I see a plastic bag or bottle, I think of that whale skeleton at Warderick Wells Cay in the Bahamas' Exuma Cays Land and Sea Park. From a distance, the skeleton looks a little bit like someone misplaced a brontosaurus on the beach. The 52-foot
50 sperm whale washed ashore in 1995 after it died from – no suspense here – ingesting plastic garbage.
The Nature Conservancy has been working in Exuma Cays through local partner Bahamas National Trust for a decade, supporting the park's staff in their
55 efforts to build nature trails, conduct research and wildlife inventories, and make the park financially self-sufficient. Managed as a no-take marine fishery reserve since 1986, the plants and animals in the park are thriving, but they can't be protected from what
60 the ocean brings in from outside the park.
The whale skeleton is a profound statement about the unintended consequences and unexpected costs of our way of life. It's a statement that needs a meaningful response, but it would be hypocritical of me to say we
65 should stop using plastic alltogether. I know I don't want to live in a world without whales, but I'm not sure that I want to live in a world without plastic either.
There might be ways to compromise. More attention is being put towards manufacturing biodegradable
70 plastics. Plastic bans or taxes are being implemented around the world. As of May 2014, there were 77 countries with plastic bag reduction policies and 133 cities in the United States with anti-plastic bag legislation according to an Earth Policy Institute
75 analysis. And the policies help.
The Portland Bureau of Planning and Sustainability found that in just one year after a plastic bag ban was put in place, the use of reusable bags increased by 304%.
80 Certainly, this isn't a silver bullet to solve our plastic addiction, but it is an important move toward a world where my convenience doesn't come at the direct cost of another creature's health.
That day in the grocery store I did the only thing
85 I could think of: took the groceries out of the plastic bags, stacked them in the cart, paid and left.
I can't change what was, but I can help change what will be. The reusable shopping bag is such a little thing, but it matters. And every one of us who bring
90 our own bags can know– from this day forward – that none of the plastic shopping bags that find their way to the ocean ever belonged to us.

Cut along the dotted lines and staple the texts together to make your own handy anthology. Make sure you keep it safe with your Workbook.

TEXTS

Text 10

I am Malala: Malala Yousafza

A year has passed since my book came out, and two years since the October morning when I was shot by the Taliban on a school bus on my way home from class. My family has been through many changes. We were plucked from our mountain valley in Swat, Pakistan, and transported to a brick house in Birmingham, England's second-biggest city. Sometimes it seems so strange to me that I want to pinch myself. I'm 17 now and one thing that has not changed is that I still don't like   5
getting up in the morning. The most astonishing thing is that it's my father whose voice wakes me up now. He gets up first every day and prepares breakfast for me, my mother and my brothers Atal and Khushal. He doesn't let his work go unnoticed, of course, going on about how he squeezes fresh juice, fries eggs, heats flatbread and takes the honey out of the cupboard. 'It's only breakfast!' I tease. For the first time in his life, he also does the shopping, although he hates doing it. The man   10
who didn't even know the price of a pint of milk is such a frequent visitor to the supermarket that he knows where everything is on the shelves! 'I've become like a woman, a true feminist!' he says, and I jokingly throw things at him.

My brothers and I then all rush off to our different schools. And so does our mother, Toor Pekai, which is truly one of the biggest changes of all. She is attending a language centre five days a   15
week to learn how to read and write, and also to speak English. My mother had no education and perhaps that was the reason she always encouraged us to go to school. 'Don't wake up like me and realise what you missed years later,' she says. She faces so many problems in her daily life, because up until now she's had difficulty communicating when she's gone shopping, or to the doctor, or the bank. Getting an education is helping her become more confident so that she can speak up outside   20
the home, not just inside with us.

A year ago I thought we would never be settled here, but now Birmingham has started to feel like home. It will never be Swat, which I miss every day, but these days, when I travel to other places and return to this new house, it does feel like home. I have even stopped thinking about the constant rain, although I laugh when my friends here complain about the heat when it's 68 or 77 degrees   25
Fahrenheit. To me that feels like spring. I am making friends at my new school, although Moniba is still my best friend and we Skype for hours at a time to catch up on everything. When she talks about parties back in Swat, I so wish I was there. Sometimes I talk to Shazia and Kainut, the other two girls who were shot on the bus and are now at Atlantic College in Wales. It is hard for them being so far away and in such a different culture, but they know they have a great opportunity to   30
fulfil their dreams of helping their communities.

The school system here is very different from the one we had in Pakistan. In my old school, I was considered 'the smart girl'. I had this idea that I would always be the smartest one and that if I worked hard or not, I would always come first. Here in the UK, the teachers expect more from their students. In Pakistan, we used to write long answers. You really could write anything you liked;   35
sometimes the examiners would get tired and give up reading part of the way through but still give you high marks! In England, the questions are often longer than the answers.

Images for questions on page 48

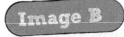

Additional image for questions on page 61

Timed test

Edexcel publishes official Sample Assessment Material on its website. This timed test has been written to help you practise what you have learned and may not be representative of a real exam paper.

In the exam, you will be given space to write in. Here, **you will need to use your own paper for your answers**.

GCSE English Language

Paper 1: Fiction and Imaginative Writing

Time: 1 hour 45 minutes

Instructions

- Answer **all** questions in Section A and **ONE** in Section B.
- You should spend about 1 hour on Section A.
- You should spend about 45 minutes on Section B.

Advice

- Read each question carefully before you start to answer it.
- Check your answers if you have time at the end.

SECTION A – Reading text

Read the text below then answer ALL the questions.

This is an extract from a novel. Silas Marner, a weaver, has built up a huge store of gold coins but they have been stolen.

Silas Marner: George Eliot

The landlord forced Marner to take off his coat, and then to sit down on a chair aloof from everyone else, in the centre of the circle and in the direct rays of the fire. The weaver, too feeble to have any distinct purpose beyond that of getting help to recover his money, submitted unresistingly. The transient[1] fears of the company[2] were now forgotten in their strong curiosity, and all faces were turned towards Silas, when the landlord, having seated himself again, said –   5

'Now then, Master Marner, what's this you've got to say – as you've been robbed? Speak out.'

'He'd better not say again it was me who robbed him,' cried Jem Rodney, hastily. 'What could I ha' done with his money? I could as easy steal the parson's surplice and wear it.'

'Hold your tongue, Jem, and let's hear what he's got to say,' said the landlord. 'Now then,   10
Master Marner.'

Silas now told his story, under frequent questioning as the mysterious character of the robbery became evident.

This strangely novel situation of opening his trouble to his Raveloe neighbours, of
sitting in the warmth of the hearth not his own, and feeling the presence of faces and   15

voices which were his nearest promise of help, had doubtless its influence on Marner, in spite of his passionate preoccupation with his loss. Our consciousness rarely registers the beginning of a growth within us any more than without us: there have been many circulations of the sap before we detect the smallest sign of the bud.

The slight suspicion with which his hearers at first listened to him gradually melted away   20
before the convincing simplicity of his distress: it was impossible for the neighbours to doubt that Marner was telling the truth, not because they were capable of arguing at once from the nature of his statements to the absence of any motive for making them falsely, but because, as Mr Macey observed, 'Folks as had the devil to back 'em were not likely to be so mushed' as poor Silas was. Rather, from the strange fact that the robber had left   25
no traces, and had happened to know the nick of time, utterly incalculable by mortal agents, when Silas would go away from home without locking his door, the more probable conclusion seemed to be that his disreputable intimacy in that quarter, if it ever existed, had been broken up, and that, in consequence, this ill turn had been done to Marner by somebody who it was quite in vain to set the constable after. Why this preternatural felon   30
should be obliged to wait till the door was left unlocked, was a question which did not present itself.

'It isn't Jem Rodney as has done this work, Master Marner,' said the landlord. 'You mustn't be a-casting your eye at poor Jem. There may be a bit of reckoning against Jem for the matter of a hare or so, if anybody was bound to keep their eyes staring open and   35
never to wink; but Jem's been a-sitting here drinking his can, like the decentest man i' the parish since before you left your house, Master Marner, by your own account.'

1: *transient* – lasting only a short time
2: *company* – group of people

1 From lines 1–7, identify a phrase which explains why the group of people are no
   longer afraid of Silas Marner   **(1 mark)**

2 From lines 8–14 give **two** reasons why the group of people are suspicious of Silas Marner.

   You may use your own words or quotations from the text.   **(2 marks)**

3 In lines 15–25, how does the writer use language and structure to show that the group
   of people believe Silas Marner's story?

   Support your views with reference to the text.   **(6 marks)**

4 In this extract, there is an attempt to create a mystery around the robbery.

   Evaluate how successfully this is achieved.

   Support your views with detailed reference to the text.   **(15 marks)**

SECTION B – Imaginative Writing

Answer ONE question. You should spend about 45 minutes on this section.

EITHER

*5 Write about a time when you, or someone you know, had to deal with a challenging experience.

   Your response could be real or imagined.

   * *Your response will be marked for the accurate and appropriate use of vocabulary,
   spelling, punctuation and grammar.*   **(40 marks)**

OR

*6 Look at the images provided.

Write about a time when you received a strange request.

Your response could be real or imagined. You may wish to base your response on one of the images.

* Your response will be marked for the accurate and appropriate use of vocabulary, spelling, punctuation and grammar.   **(40 marks)**

Timed test

Edexcel publishes official Sample Assessment Material on its website. This timed test has been written to help you practise what you have learned and may not be representative of a real exam paper.

In the exam, you will be given space to write in. Here, **you will need to use your own paper for your answers**.

GCSE English Language

Paper 2: Non-fiction and Transactional Writing

Time: 2 hours

Instructions

- Answer **all** questions in Section A and **ONE** in Section B.
- You should spend about 1 hour and 15 minutes on Section A.
- You should spend about 45 minutes on Section B.

Advice

- Read each question carefully before you start to answer it.
- Check your answers if you have time at the end.

SECTION A – Reading texts

Read Text 1 below and answer Questions 1–3 on the question paper.

Text 1

This text is adapted from an article called 'Is taking your kids on holiday good?' originally published on the website www.parenting.co.uk.

Take your kids on holiday!

The destination is unimportant: children love going on holiday. And going away as a whole family can provide valuable quality time and memories that will last children their whole lives. The type of holiday — whether it's cosy camping in a back garden or death-defying rollercoasters somewhere exotic — will depend on the age of the children, how many days can be spent away, and the budget. But really the price is as unimportant as the   5
place — all that matters is that the family spends time together in a different way to their usual day-to-day lives. This means no television or internet — and no chattering mobile phones!

Who hasn't been on a holiday where everything went wrong? A disaster holiday. But these are the most memorable. Seeing their parents relaxing or being as silly as children   10
can bring the most comfort to a family. Knowing that, despite the most unimaginable problems, 'everything will be alright' can help children feel safe and secure — this feeling remains after the holiday has ended.

Holidays are also a chance to experience something new. Foods, people and activities can be vastly different, and a child used to trying something new on holiday will try something   15
new at home too. Actually experiencing new things is important: children can read about the vast blue ocean stretching endlessly away from them, the impossible heights of

enormous towering mountains or the repeating regular rhythm of a steam locomotive, but nothing compares to being there themselves. And experiencing it together can strengthen family bonds. 20

A break away can also offer just that – a break. Like adults, children need a chance to relax so they can learn to schedule time for fun into their lives before they go back to working in a more productive way. It also helps them to see that while work and school are important, enjoying life and spending time with your family are important too.

A vacation cannot offer everything children need to be successful in life, but it is 25 important in its own way. Family activities — whether they are building a campfire, canoeing or even arts and crafts — give children a chance to experience different cultures and try something new. They offer a chance to bond with family members, have a break from life and just be silly; experiences that will have a positive impact throughout their whole lives. 30

What do You Think? Follow Parenting.co.uk (2012)

Read Text 2 below and answer Questions 4–6 on the question paper.

The text comes from an article written by Joanna Moorhead, entitled 'Would you take your child on holiday during term time?'

Would you take your child on holiday during term time?

As a father's Facebook rant about 'rip-off' travel costs during school holidays goes viral, we ask two parents to argue the case for and against taking children on holiday in term time. Then it's over to you. Tell us what you'd do in the comments below.

Why I'm taking my child out of school for a holiday (by *Anonymous*)

This half-term, my family and I are leaving the country for a much-needed break. To save 5 around £800, I will be taking my child out of school before the term officially ends. I have not sought permission from the head teacher. Nor will I. In the light of the recent case of the Sutherlands in Milton Keynes, what would once have seemed a perfectly reasonable request has taken on a politicised significance, forcing me into the inconsiderate-parent-more-interested-in-a-sunny-holiday-than-my-child's-education camp. But that is to 10 simplify a hugely complicated set of issues about what education should consist of, the role of the state in dictating family activities and the value of travel (abroad or at home).

Firstly, I genuinely don't feel my child (aged 4) will be disadvantaged by one or two days out of school. Second, and controversially, I don't feel the school will be disadvantaged either. I know how the argument goes – if everyone behaved like me we'd be in a sorry 15 state with half-empty classrooms. But, really, would we? Aren't those who shout the loudest about the need for attendance the ones who are rich enough for term-time holidays never to be an issue?

I do feel guilty, but only for families who don't have the same financial resources as we do, so can't have a holiday at all, term time or not. I can't imagine any teacher devaluing the 20 chance to learn a few words of a foreign language in situ, to see geology in action by playing on black sand, or start to understand basic engineering principles by looking at how planes fly. For us, the physical, intellectual and social advantages of travel would not be financially possible if we waited until the school holidays. Of course, I agree that attendance (most of the time) is vital but so is family harmony, unfrazzled parents, time to read or explore the 25 world without the pressures of day-to-day life. Until travel companies offer more reasonable prices during school holidays, families like mine will continue to take their children out of school. Perhaps we should go easy on parents who value spending time with their children in a new and stimulating environment over Ofsted attendance targets.

Why I'll never take my children out of school for a holiday (by *Anonymous*)

As chief holiday-planner in our household of six, I could be a lot richer – and/or my children 30
could have seen a lot more of the world – if I'd fished them out of school, or even just shaved
a few days off the beginning or end of term here and there. Instead, over the last 16 years
while we've had school-age kids, we've kept our holidays religiously within the vacation dates:
and as my youngest child is still only 11, we've got another seven years of the same ahead.

It's irksome[1], because there are huge financial savings to be made. Also, who wants to 35
be on the beach in August, when it's packed and baking hot, when June and September
(which is when my husband and I always holidayed in those dim and distant days before
our eldest was born) are so less crowded, and the temperature more agreeable?

So why not just flout the system? Well, it all comes down to respect. Like all parents, I
have occasional issues with aspects of my children's education: but on the whole, I aim to 40
support the primary and comprehensive schools where they are, and have been, pupils.
And part of the way I show my respect and support is by following the rules: and rule
number one is, make sure your child is in school when he or she should be there.

So many parents seem not to realise that the reason their kids don't work hard, or play
truant, or get into trouble with their teachers, is connected to the fact that they have an 45
à la carte[2] attitude to rules themselves. If you want your child to stick two fingers up at
their teachers, to think education doesn't matter, or to skimp on revising for an exam,
then go ahead and take them out of school so you can jet off on an exciting holiday for
a fortnight. What you are role-modelling by your behaviour is your belief that rules are
for other people, not for you; and your kids will pick up on that very, very quickly. 50

And here's another thing. My eldest, post-uni[3], is currently saving up to go to Asia on a
gap year. Because travel is for life; but school is only for childhood, and as holiday-loving
parents we need to remember that.

1: *irksome* – irritating
2: *à la carte* – French phrase translated to 'according to the menu', meaning to choose which parts you like
3: *post-uni* – after university

Joanna Moorhead
The Guardian, **29th January, 2014**

SECTION A – Reading

Read Text 1. Then answer Questions 1–3.

You should spend about 1 hour 15 minutes on the WHOLE of Section A (Questions 1–7)

1 In lines 4–12, identify **two** reasons why family holidays might having lasting benefits
   for children.   **(2 marks)**

2 Give **one** example from lines 11–15 of how the writer uses language to create an image
   of an impressive holiday experience.   **(2 marks)**

3 Analyse how the writer uses language and structure to engage the readers.
   Support you views with detailed reference to the text.   **(6 marks)**

Read Text 2. Then answer Questions 4–6

4 Identify the saving made by taking a child out of school shortly before the term ends.   **(1 mark)**

5 In lines 10–14, how does the writer use language to suggest that education is not a
   straightforward experience?   **(1 mark)**

6 In the newspaper article, there is an attempt to engage the reader by exploring the
   different perspectives on holidays taken in term or school holiday time.

   Evaluate how successfully this is achieved.

   Support your views with detailed reference to the text.   **(15 marks)**

**Question 7 is about Text 1 and Text 2. Answer both parts of the question. Refer to both
texts in your answers.**

7 **(a)** The two texts show the points of view of different parents.

   What similarities do the parents in Text 1 and Text 2 share in these texts?

   Use evidence from both texts to support your answer.   **(6 marks)**

   (b) Compare how the writers of Text 1 and Text 2 present their ideas and perspectives
   about taking time out for family holidays.

   Support your ideas with detailed reference to the text.   **(14 marks)**

Section B – Transactional writing

Answer ONE question. You should spend about 45 minutes on this section.

EITHER

*8 Write an article for your school magazine in which you explore the advantages and
   disadvantages of taking holidays during school time.

   You could:
   • describe the issues relating to taking holidays in term time
   • explain any benefits of families taking a holiday together
   • give your views on how much is gained by taking a holiday

   as well as any other ideas you might have.

   *Your response will be marked for the accurate and appropriate use of vocabulary,
   spelling, punctuation and grammar.*   **(40 marks)**

   OR

*9 Write a review of a family activity. It could be a weekend break, a longer holiday or a visit to a place..

You could write about:

- the reasons why the activity appealed to you as a family
- how far the activity was regarded as successful by all who participated
- whether or not you consider this an experience to be recommended to others

as well as any other ideas you might have.

* Your response will be marked for the accurate and appropriate use of vocabulary, spelling, punctuation and grammar.

(40 marks)

Answers

SECTION A: READING

1. Planning your exam time

1 Paper 1: 10 minutes. Paper 2: **15 minutes**

2 About two minutes (Note: you could spend less time on your answer to save time for checking your work.)

3 You should refer to lines **1–3**.

4 About 15 minutes

5 Two (both) texts

6 All options should be circled.

2. Reading texts explained

1 (a) Answer provided on page 2

  (b) For example: The words suggest that the people in the house are troubled and uneasy. The words **'bad feeling' suggest that the people in the house were not happy. The words 'oppressor' and 'usurper' suggest that relationships have changed for the worse since Heathcliff has arrived. The words 'he grew bitter with brooding' create an impression that he is spending all his time thinking about how things have changed and he resents that.**

2 My family has been through many changes. We were plucked from our mountain valley in Swat, Pakistan, and transported to a brick house in Birmingham, England's second-biggest city. Sometimes it seems so strange to me that I want to pinch myself. I'm 17 now and one thing that has not changed is that I still don't like getting up in the morning. The most astonishing thing is that it's my father whose voice wakes me up now. He gets up first every day and prepares breakfast for me, my mother and my brothers Atal and Khushal. For example: The words 'plucked' and 'transported' give the impression that the narrator's move from Swat to Birmingham was unexpected. Malala's life **changed a lot when she moved from Pakistan to Birmingham. She felt the change was sudden as they were 'plucked' from their home. The writer also uses 'transported' to show they had little/no choice.**

Despite the upheaval of moving, **Malala finds it 'so strange' she wants to 'pinch' herself as it does not seem real. She uses the word 'astonishing' to show how her father has taken on a new role in the household and 'astonishing' suggests it is unexpected and has amazed them.**

From 'mountain valley' to 'brick house' suggests **moving from an expansive rural area to a built-up urban area.**

3. Reading questions explained 1

1 AO1(a)

2 AO1(a)

3 AO1(b)

4 AO3

4. Reading questions explained 2

Great Expectations

Example notes could include:

- 'black velvet', 'silver basket' 'cake and wine' and 'gold stars' all point to excessive luxury and get more lavish throughout the extract – the exaggeration is humorous

- the imagery of 'immense' dogs fighting for 'veal cutlets out of a silver basket' is amusing – the idea that four dogs would be eating such luxurious food out of such a delicate dish is entertaining for the reader

- Pip's response to being under pressure makes the reader think he is going to break at any moment. He is 'reckless under torture' which builds up the tension and the humour in the extract

- the setting Pip describes is comical, the idea of having a large 'black velvet coach' inside a room, and by stating that there 'were no horses to it' is highly entertaining

- based on the examples found in the text, Dickens is successful at showing humour when the narrator has to account for his visit to Miss Havisham.

Notes from a Small Island

Example notes could include:

- the very poor weather conditions which become more and more exaggerated (the rain is 'driving', the metaphor 'bullets of shiny rain' showing force of raindrops)

- references to descriptions of how soaked he is ('soaked through', 'shedding water', 'decanting water', 'drippingly')

- amusing situation of being in a 'smothering' warmth that 'makes your glasses steam' – the fact he can't see is comical

- he gives impression of a much-changed Bournemouth overly negative connotations (the pedestrian network of subways are 'befuddling' and you have to be 'like a gopher' to see anything – the animal imagery is unexpected and, therefore, humorous

- uses humour (sarcasm, 'No, my ship sank' and the comical name 'Mr Brylcreem')

- based on the examples found in the text, Bill Bryson is successful at entertaining the reader with his personal account of arriving at the hotel.

5. Reading the questions

1 (a) Answer provided on page 5

  (b) 'give'

2 Paper 1, Question 3: one text; lines 19–29; 'language and structure', 'Heathcliff's behaviour and attitude'; about 12 minutes.

Paper 2, Question 6: one text; whole extract; 'family felt', 'Evaluate'; 15 minutes.

Paper 2, Question 7 (a): two texts; both texts; 'women's lives', 'need to change', 'similarities'; about 6 minutes. (Note: The calculation for the length of time to spend on each answer is based on about 2 minutes per mark for Paper 1 and about 1 minute per mark for Paper 2. You could choose to spend slightly less time per mark to save time for checking your work.)

6. Skimming for the main idea or theme

1 (a) Answer provided on page 6

  (b) For example: The closing sentence suggests **that the main idea is that there is no research to support the idea that fidget spinners will help people cope with anxiety; it may also suggest that they don't really help.**

2 (a) For example: It suggests that the article is showing **the reader that it is easy to get the fidget spinners/ they are readily available and shows how very popular they have become.**

  (b) At the beginning of the article **the idea seems to be that they are very popular. By the end of this section of the article we understand that they vary in price and that their value is questionable.**

115

3 (a) • Answer provided on page 6
  • Small devices
    • Marketed as an aid for ADHD, autism and anxiety
    • No evidence they do help and may do harm
  (b) For example: Fidget spinners are small. They are being marketed for ADHD, autism and anxiety but they might not help.
  (c) For example: Fidget spinners are small but popular devices. They are being marketed for various conditions but there is no evidence whether they help or may do harm.

7. Annotating the texts

1 (a) A, B, C, D and F
  (b) The sentences get longer to reflect the narrator's building worries.
  (c) The annotation that does not help answer the question is E because **it is about Mr Pumblechook and not about the narrator.**

2 Answers should include four or five annotations showing how successfully the writer shows the bullying of the narrator. For example, you may identify explicit and implicit meaning and refer to the following:

3 Setting
  • Pip has returned home which should be a safe place, but instead is one of conflict. One that he wants to 'escape' from
  • Pip describes the room at Miss Havisham's as having 'no daylight' and instead says it was 'all lighted up with candles' – implies a desire for escapism from his home
Theme (conflict)
  • 'I wish you had him always' to have control – they are joining forces against him
  • 'both stared at me' – he is intimidated
  • 'reckless witness under the torture'
Theme (power)
  • 'applying the screw' suggests that Mr Pumblechook is putting pressure on the narrator, also suggests torture
  • 'conceitedly', 'this is the way to have him': demonstrating they want control over narrator
Ideas
  • The 'perfectly frantic' narrator is in distress/terrified
  • The contrast and conflict between youth and age
  • The contrast between light and dark, real and imagined
  • 'I escaped' suggests being with them is an ordeal
Events
  • 'they both stared at me' and 'I stared at them' is a moment of tension between the characters – it is two against one
  • Mr Pumblechook 'folding his arms tight on his chest' is showing an aggressive position against Pip.

8. Putting it into practice

1 (a) and (b) Answers should include four or five annotated words or phrases. For example:
  • 'lighting up' – this conversation about Fred makes Mary passionately angry
  • 'I wonder' – Rosamond is in disbelief about Mary's opinion on Fred
  • 'You always' – shows they have had this discussion before
  • 'You make me feel very uncomfortable' – shows the effect of this conversation on Rosamond.

2 For example: The writer uses language and structure throughout this section to show the effect Fred has on Mary and Rosamond. They contradict each other, for example, 'I wonder that you can defend Fred' , 'I don't defend him'. Most of what we learn is in the structure of the dialogue, but we are also provided with narrative detail, for example, Rosamond is 'inclined to push this point', suggesting that she will not let something go. The discussion causes an angry reaction from Mary – 'lighting up' which shows that Fred is causing a major disagreement at this point.

9. Putting it into practice

1 Answer should include four or five annotated phrases. For example: he describes the very poor weather conditions (the rain is 'driving', the metaphor 'bullets of shiny rain' showing force of raindrops, he is soaked and is 'shedding water', he 'decanted several ounces of water', use of the adverb, 'drippingly'); he gives impression of a much-changed Bournemouth overly negative connotations (the pedestrian network of subways are 'befuddling' and you have to be 'like a gopher' to see anything – the animal imagery is unexpected and, therefore, humorous); amusing situation of being in a 'smothering' warmth that 'makes your glasses steam' – the fact he can't see is comical; references to descriptions of how soaked he is ('soaked through', 'shedding water', 'decanting water'); uses humour (sarcasm, 'No, my ship sank' and the comical name 'Mr Brylcreem').

2 For example: Bill Bryson is successful at entertaining the reader with his personal account of arriving at the hotel. He convinces the reader, through a combination of sarcasm and exaggeration, that even the most unpromising and mundane events can be humorous.

3 Example paragraphs may include the following.
  • When Bill Bryson writes of Bournemouth, it could be inferred that he does not have a completely positive opinion, but he still uses humorous imagery to describe his disconcerting surroundings. For example, the new pedestrian system is 'befuddling' and leaves pedestrians like 'gophers' popping up 'every few minutes', the animal imagery is unexpected and, therefore, humorous.
  • Bill Bryson spends much of the extract exaggerating the extent to which he is soaked through, from 'shedding water' and 'decanted several ounces of water' to use of the adverb, 'drippingly' – this exaggeration creates a build-up of tension as he is desperate to get inside the hotel. As a result, the reader is compelled to read further and to find out if he does get dry.
  • When Bill Bryson states 'the only thing to be said for Bournemouth', he is suggesting that that there is little else going for it and that he is not impressed. Similarly, he is unenthusiastic about the receptionist who is not 'attending' his 'words closely', and gets his name wrong with the amusing 'Mr Brylcreem'. He describes her as having a 'cheerily bean-sized brain', suggested by her reaction to his sarcastic answer, 'No, my ship sank and I had to swim the last seven miles' – the fact that the ridiculousness of his answer is ignored by the receptionist is entertaining for the reader.
  • Bill Bryson's delight with the room at the end of the extract, 'I was very happy', surprises the reader and is even more entertaining – his excitement is humorously over-the-top as a response to the mediocre room.

10. Explicit information and ideas
1 'There was a vague uneasiness'
2 Broken DVD case
3 (a) maturity
   (b) taking responsibility
4 2017

11. Implicit ideas
1 (a) Answer given on page 11.
   (b) Explicit
   (c) Implicit
2 Answers should include at least three ideas, for example:
   (a) 'not encouraging to strangers'
   (b) 'no pity for weakness'
   (c) 'almost oppressive generosity'

12. Inference
1 Annotations could include:
   'perfectly frantic'
   'reckless witness'
   'would have told them anything'
   'added this saving clause'
   'in the moment of rejecting'
   'wild thoughts of harnessing'
2 For example: The extract suggests that the narrator **is finding the interview traumatic so will tell them anything to ease the pressure.**
   Quotation: **'I was perfectly frantic'**
3 For example: The narrator is presented as someone who is not used to telling lies, shown by the words **'I think of myself with amazement'. This suggests that he is normally honest.**

13. Interpreting information and ideas
1 (a) 'absolutely'– completely, utterly
   (b) 'necessary'– vital, essential
   (c) 'combatants' – fighters, opponents
2 (a) The word 'insolent' suggests Heathcliff's lack of respect.
   (b) The word 'insensible' shows Heathcliff does not care about the feelings of others.

14. Using evidence
1 For example: The writer is very affected by the skeleton of the whale because the whale had been killed by eating plastics. This makes the death 'profound' because of what it is telling us about how plastic is killing marine wildlife. The writer realises that as human beings this is not what we wanted to happen – this is 'unintended'. She uses the phrase 'unexpected costs' which suggests that **the problems that plastics would cause for wildlife had not been anticipated. She suggests that as human beings we did not want this to happen to the whales, and uses the word 'unintended' to illustrate this point.**
2 For example: The writer knows that we cannot alter what has happened in the past but she feels that we can **make a difference in the future. She believes that reusing bags seems like a small action but collectively those who use their own bags will know that they will not be responsible for any other bags found in the sea.**

15. Point – Evidence – Explain
1 For example:
   Make your point: The writer uses several verbs to show the type of care that parents gave their teenagers as children.

Provide evidence to support your point: For example, 'nursed', **'protected' would be crucial when an adult was looking after a baby or small child and 'appealed' and 'begged' suggests a parent looking after a toddler.**
   Introduce your explanation: This gives the impression that **teenagers should not expect and do not need the far-reaching care and attention that parents gave them as children.**
2 For example, she uses the words, **'every** benefit', **'dearest treasure', 'selfish ego'.**

16. Putting it into practice
1 (a) 'I call Fred conceited.'
   (b) For example: Thinking 'horrid' is 'so unsuitable a word' suggests Rosamond takes being a lady very seriously. She looks down on Fred because 'He is so idle', showing by contrast that she thinks of herself as serious and purposeful.
2 For example:
   The main device used by the writer to show the disagreement between Mary and Rosamond is through the dialogue. In response to a point made by Rosamond, for example, Mary refutes her logic by stating 'It does not follow' which is a direct contradiction of her friend's point. When Rosamond refers to the money spent on Fred's education, the writer uses the adverb 'dryly' to describe how Mary responds. This suggests that she finds the conversation amusing and she may even disapprove of the reference to money.
   You may also refer to the narrative description to show that Rosamond does not know when to stop and Mary finds this initially amusing but later it makes her angry.

17. Putting it into practice
1 Answers could include these key points:
   • The writer begins with first person narrative about a trip to the supermarket where she finds she has forgotten her bags. She uses familiar references to a familiar situation: 'reusable shopping bags,' 'grocery store', 'two antsy kids.'
   • She broadens out this reference by linking the plastic bags with the dead sperm whale. She uses hypophora to connect the plastic bags with the whale.
   • 'PLASTICS: 1, MARINE MAMMALS: 0'
     She condenses the theme of the article into this subheading which adds impact and which makes the words stand out from rest of the article.
   • Reference to a variety of techniques used by the writer, including listing, repetition and rhetorical devices such as alliteration: 'circling in the current'.
   • Reference to use of facts and figures, e.g. '90% of seabirds', the impact of plastics on nature and the conclusion to the text, giving the way we can help.

18. Word classes
1 Examples could include:
   • noun – taxes, counties, bag, cities, United States, reduction, legislation, policies, names of organisations/institutions, year, place
   • adjective – reusable, plastic
   • verb – compromise, being, put, manufacturing, help, found, use, increased
   • preposition – towards, around, with, anti, after, in, by.
2 For example: The modal verb 'might' suggests **that it is a possibility but not definite/guaranteed.**
3 For example: Adjective: broad (chest) suggests he is an imposing man with strong physique, a strong physical presence.

Verbs: encumbered suggests a burden of some sort, and Elizabeth is free from this and free to simply observe what is going on.

Verbs: regarded/looked at/assessed suggests that Elizabeth is neutral and just looking at the mayor with interest.

19. Connotations

1 (a) gleaming palaces of comfort = answer given on page 19

glowing beckoningly = shining in a way that invites you in, like a moth to a light

smothering warmth = answer given on page 19

decanted = emptied out water

attractively priced at £26 B&B = a reasonably priced but very ordinary bed and breakfast

(b) For example:

The phrase 'gleaming palaces of comfort' suggests places which are height of luxury and comfort. The adjective 'gleaming' **suggests that they are so clean that they reflect the light. 'Glowing' picks up on this but could be connoted to suggest that it is a beacon to draw in the travellers. The adverb 'beckoningly' also suggest that it is inviting and luring in the guests.**

2 For example:

(a) Heathcliff is 'sullen' which suggests that he makes no attempt to be friendly or grateful, he just takes what he wants.

(b) 'Indulgence' suggests that the master (benefactor) gives Heathcliff what he wants all the time and also suggests that he spoils him.

20. Figurative language

1 The metaphor 'a reckless witness under the torture' suggests that the narrator feels **desperate and is finding the experience of being questioned agonising.**

This suggests to the reader that **as a consequence, the narrator is becoming increasingly outrageous in what he tells them, which could lead to a lot of trouble.**

2 For example:

(a) The writer uses the simile 'he was as uncomplaining as a lamb'.

(b) On first reading, this suggests that he was gentle and undemanding. However, it sounds sarcastic when we hear it is 'hardness' that makes him uncomplaining.

3 For example:

(a) The writer personifies 'time' as a magician who has done much here to ensure the mayor's success.

(b) This suggests that, although not actually magical, there is something unworldly and unexpected about the change the narrator is witnessing.

21. Creation of character

1 For example:

Use of dialogue:

Heathcliff's words, **'You must exchange horses ... I don't like mine' show that he believes he deserves only the best as a matter of right. Hindley's words, calling Heathcliff a 'dog' show he looks down on him.**

Use of action:

Heathcliff's actions, **(threatening Hindley with violence) are shown to be intimidating and are used by Heathcliff to get his own way, namely blackmail. Hindley reacts with a childish gesture, 'put out his tongue'.**

Use of description:

Heathcliff is described as being very active in the extract, trying to provoke a reaction. However, he achieves this through words whereas Hindley's reaction is described in a more physical way. Hindley sticks out his tongue, cuffs Heathcliff around the ear and throws the iron weight at him.

2 For example:

Heathcliff is aggressive and threatening, uses his words to taunt and provoke Hindley to violence. However, the line, he 'staggered up immediately, breathless and white' shifts the power back from Heathcliff to Hindley, as Heathcliff displays shock at having the iron weight thrown at him.

3 For example:

Point: Hindley is **shown to quickly become more violent in the final paragraph.**

Evidence: This is shown by **him beginning with calling Heathcliff names, 'off dog!' and then threatening Heathcliff with an iron weight.**

Explanation: This suggests that **the aggression has worsened from name-calling to serious violence as the blow caused Heathcliff to fall, making him 'breathless and white'.**

22. Creating atmosphere

1 The personification of time as 'the magician' creates a mood **of the unexpected – there is something almost unreal about the encounter.**

Other possible responses could be, for example:

- connotations of shame and intimidation – 'she shrank back' creates a mood of distress
- pattern of three – 'go – pass away – die' – the bluntness of her words emphasises the tone of extreme hopelessness
- there is a mood of abandonment – we can infer that Susan is so 'moved' by what she sees, that she forgets her daughter is there
- the tension is broken when the daughter 'whispered' to her mother – this breaks the spell the mother is under.

2 In the extract, the mayor is wearing an 'evening suit'. The adjectives used by the writer create an atmosphere of **wealth and excess and this is connoted by the references to the 'frilled' shirt, 'jewelled studs' and the 'heavy gold chain' of office. He appears to have had the choice of two glasses of wine, but he chooses to drink water. Susan remembers him as wearing coarse cloth of the peasant stock and eating an inexpensive dish of 'furmity'. This contrasts with his clothes, his surroundings and the suggestion of fine dining.**

3 Overall, the writer creates an atmosphere of **power and wealth by choosing language to suggest success such as 'jewelled' and contrasts this with his previous circumstances.**

23. Narrative voice

1 A – Extract 3: *Wuthering Heights*

B – Extract 1: *Middlemarch*

C – Extract 2: *Great Expectations*

2 The first person narrator involves the reader by **sharing with them what he was about to tell them next, either the 'balloon in the yard' or the 'bear in the brewery' so although the characters do not hear this, the reader knows what he might have said and is entertained by these possibilities.**

24. Putting it into practice

1 Answers could include these key points:
- Heathcliff issues the command 'You must' which suggests that ultimately, Hindley will have no choice.
- Hindley uses the minor sentence 'Off dog!' in his dialogue. This way of addressing Heathcliff is disrespectful – by using the name of an animal, Hindley shows how he does not regard Heathcliff as being human.
- The words, 'he grew bitter with brooding' foreshadow the later tension in the extract, where Hindley acts violently against Heathcliff.
- Hindley's actions of putting out his tongue and cuffing Heathcliff do not stop Heathcliff from pursuing what he wants and he threatens Hindley with violence as well: 'you'll get them again with interest' although, in contrast, Heathcliff will rely on someone else to carry out the violence.
- The simile, 'as uncomplaining as a lamb' earlier in the extract ensures that the reader feels sympathy with Heathcliff when Hindley is violent towards him later.
- Hindley carries out the threat but Heathcliff is prevented from going to the master for 'full revenge' by Mrs Dean.

25. Rhetorical devices 1

1 For example, four of the following:
- pattern of three – 'plastic, plastic, plastic' (also repetition)
- lists – 'plastic bags, plastic cups, plastic sheeting, plastic bottles'
- alliteration – 'circling the current'
- colloquial language – Answer given on page 25
- hypophora – 'The connection between the two? The plastic bags.'

2 For example: The writer uses a list to emphasise how much plastic we use in the world: 'plastic bags, plastic cups, plastic sheeting'. As it is part of her wider article about plastic, it makes the reader aware that this is a big problem. The writer also **uses colloquial language 'antsy kids' to make the familiar situation of shopping with children more vivid, something that readers would experience or witness. This is conversational and engages the reader before the writer moves into the main purpose of her text: the impact of plastics on marine wildlife.**

26. Rhetorical devices 2

1 Examples could include:
- repetition: the words 'militant' and 'ask questions'
- emotive language: 'brutally-ill-used'
- contrast: 'eight years' and '24 hours' versus 'custom' and 'time-honoured' (short time periods versus long traditions that could be in place for many years)

2 For example:
'militant': **suggests proactive, probably aggressive behaviour, suggesting that the women along with Emmeline Pankhurst use violent methods to present their case.**
'questions': **in the context of her point, questions are seemingly harmless when the men ask them. However, when the women in Mrs Pankhurst's cause ask them, they are evicted from the meeting. So, questions have different connotations depending on who is asking them.**

3 The writer refers to two babies who are both very hungry but behave differently. One is very loud and the other is very patient. She then goes on to explain **that the one who makes the most fuss is the one who will be** fed first. The quiet baby will not be fed first because s/he is not making life unpleasant. She uses this to illustrate her point that being quiet will not get any results, but drawing attention to the issue through action will.

4 Pattern of three: **'you have to make more noise than anybody else, you have to make yourself more obtrusive than anybody else, you have to fill all the papers more than anybody else'. She uses this device to emphasise what you need to do for your cause. She identifies the need for 'noise', being 'obtrusive' and publicity: 'fill all the papers'. She uses the comparative 'more' to suggest that your campaign must be more obvious than anyone else's.**
Metaphor: **'you cannot make omelettes without breaking eggs' suggests that you have to be prepared for some damage before something good can come out of the situation. So, eggs have to be broken or action needs to be taken to obtain the desired outcome. This justifies the action to the reader.**

27. Fact, opinion and expert evidence

1 Something known to be true; Fact; Malala Yousafzai was born 12 July 1997
The opinion of a person or group with special knowledge about a subject; Expert evidence; You should improve your diet and do more exercise to give you the best chance of living longer.
Something a person believes that may or may not be true; Opinion; Ed Sheeran is superior to all other musicians.

2 (a) B
 (b) C
 (c) A

3 (a) For example: Fact: 'there is no proof to support this claim'
 Opinion: 'the devices (are regularly marketed to) provide increased focus and stress relief'
 Expert evidence: 'many children with ADHD benefit from some forms of movement'
 (b) Fact: **the writer presents the lack of evidence as 'proof' to suggest that any benefits of fidget spinners are open to question.**
 Opinion: **it is widely believed that the device has benefits and is marketed by those who believe it has benefits, but this is not supported by evidence.**
 Expert evidence: **the writer uses the expert view that some forms of movement help but use of the word 'some' suggests research is ongoing and further supports the idea that there is insufficient evidence. It also suggests that if the expert is cautious about what can help, those marketing the product are doing so without really knowing its impact.**

28. Identifying sentence types

1 (a) single-clause sentence
 (b) multi-clause sentence (subordinate)
 (c) multi-clause sentence (coordinate)
 (d) minor sentence

2 For example: *Multi-clause sentence (subordinate)*
'By the time I reached the East Cliff, a neighbourhood of medium-sized hotels perched high above a black sea, I was soaked through and muttering.'
Single-clause sentence 'The only thing to be said for Bournemouth is that you are certainly spoiled for choice with hotels.'
Multi-clause sentence (coordinate) 'I decanted several ounces of water from my sleeve and asked for a single room for two nights.'

3 *Multi-clause sentence (subordinate)*
'By the time I reached the East Cliff…'
– builds up layers of description to give a really vivid sense of the location.
Single-clause sentence 'The only thing to be said for Bournemouth…'
– very blunt, short sentence when compared with the other sentences. It is used to really make the point that Bournemouth hasn't got a lot going for it.
Multi-clause sentence (coordinate) 'I decanted several ounces of water from my sleeve and asked for a single room for two nights.'
– describes two unrelated actions in a factual way which creates momentum.

29. Commenting on sentence types

1 For example: The narrator uses **multi-clause sentences** to describe **her feelings and to link her feelings with what is happening in life.** So she acknowledges it will 'never be Swat' but uses clauses to indicate her travels and her return to her house with the final clause 'it does feel like home.' She uses a single clause sentence to present her view of British weather, following a multi-clause sentence to explore how her British friends regard the weather. Her single clause sentence is her response and opinion: 'To me, it feels like spring.' She uses these structures to present her feelings about her friends back home. A multi-clause sentence is used to present communicating with her friend.

2 For example: The writer starts the paragraph with a short question to show that Elizabeth is feeling **puzzled.** This is immediately followed by a multi-clause sentence to describe her interaction with her mother as Elizabeth wants to know answers. She follows this with **a question 'Does he seem to you not likely to befriend us? In this, she combines asking her mother's view with his potential friendliness.**
The writer uses a single-clause sentence to build up Elizabeth's excitement 'And how his diamond studs shine!' This is followed by **a multi-clause subordinate sentence in which Elizabeth lists the possible different fates for the man who is a successful mayor.**

3 For example: Elizabeth asks a question in a single-clause sentence, showing how she challenges her mother, 'Why should you feel so afraid of him?' The single clause makes the message clear. She answers the unspoken question of her own feelings by the single clause, 'I am not at all.' The writer uses the multi-clause coordinate sentence to indicate Elizabeth's intention to visit and his possible reaction, using a dash between the clauses: 'I'll call upon him – he can but say he don't own such remote kin.'

30. Structure: non-fiction

1 For example: The writer begins her article with direct address to the reader. This has the effect of encouraging the reader to read on because they can relate to the 'common complaint' they are being asked about.

2 (a) calls to action
(b) For example: The effect of the extract is persuasive and the writer wants to effect change so chooses to end in this way.

3 Byington uses statistics to support her argument that the use of plastics is destroying wildlife. She refers to 90% of seabirds who have 'ingested' plastic and it is implied that this is linked to the cause of death. She later starts to write about possible solutions when she

suggests we start with our own action: using reusable bags. She refers to the 'silver bullet' which is part of folklore in that it will stop a werewolf permanently. Here, she uses it to suggest that we do not have the final answer to the problem but it is a step forward.

31. Structure: fiction

1 The words 'bitter brooding' suggest that Hindley **resents what is happening and that this is long-lasting as he is 'brooding' which also suggests that he is always thinking about the situation and that he has negative feelings about what is happening. This suggests that he will not be able to let this situation go and would be unable to move on in the future.**

2 The extract begins with Mr Pumblechook demanding answers from the narrator. He commands a response: 'Boy! What like is Miss Havisham?' and he has negative body language of folded arms. The narrator uses figurative language, describing Mr Pumblechook 'applying the screw'. This suggests that what is going to follow is going to be unpleasant for the narrator. The structure of the text is presented through dialogue and the sequence of exchanges between the narrator and his interrogators. The narrator realises that Mr Pumblechook has never seen Miss Havisham who is not 'tall and dark' as described in response to the question. As she is 'nothing of the kind' the reader knows that the only character in the conversation who can give an accurate description of her is the narrator.

3 The short extract builds up to the final paragraph because the narrator shares with the reader his awareness that Mr Pumblechook who 'winked assent' rather than tell an outright lie, has never seen Miss Havisham. The narrator in the short extract gives a false description of her appearance. The reader knows that his interrogators are unrelenting and this, combined with the narrator's discomfort, leads to the narrator telling lies which become increasingly ridiculous as the extract continues. The writer uses the lies to structure the writing, ending with the narrator's escape before his lies become so outrageous that his dishonesty is discovered.

32. Putting it into practice

1 For example:
- The writer uses the adverb 'mildly' to describe Rosamond's temperament. This shows that she is staying calm although Mary is angry.
- The writer uses a multi-clause sentence to show Mary as on the defensive regarding a possible marriage with Fred – she is almost going into too much detail so she is not as believable. Then her speech ends with a single clause sentence, 'He certainly has never asked me.' This is designed to make her denial of the situation emphatic.
- The repetition of the words 'you are always' spoken by both Mary and Rosamond, emphasises their difference rather than their similarities.
- The short rhetorical question 'I?' is used for effect and shows Rosamond's outrage.
- Rosamond always refers to Mary by her name, which shows a certain need for power over her.
- The next sequence of sentences are single clauses to show that the exchange between the friends is becoming angry.
- The extract closes with an attempt by Mary to close down the discussion with a multi-clause coordinate

in which the clauses are separated by dashes: 'There is the bell – I think we must go down.'

33. Putting it into practice

1 Answers could include the following key points:
Language:
- temporal references 'one year' and 'two years' create a sense of time passing and context
- verbs such as 'plucked' which suggests no choice and 'transported' to show the family were passive
- contrasting descriptions: 'mountain valley' of their former home, contrasting with 'brick house in Birmingham' showing that they have exchanged rural life in another country for city life in England
- use of language to show it is all different: 'strange', 'pinch myself', 'astonishing'
- language for emphasis, 'truly' referring to the change relating to her mother
- use of superlative, 'smartest' to show how life has changed for Malala in terms of where she is in the English education system, in comparison with Swat.

Structure:
- multi-clause sentences are used to describe Swat and England in the same sentence, which helps the reader to understand the pull the writer feels to both places
- uses a lot of exclamation points throughout the extract which help the reader to feel the writer's sense of surprise at her new situation in England
- starts with reminder of why they came to England
- moves on to how life has changed for all the family
- discusses how they settle, friends at home and in UK
- ends with comparison of school systems and teacher expectations.

34. Handling two texts

1 Assessment objective 3
2 (a) Paper 2
  (b) Question 7 (b)
  (c) Question 7 (a)
  (d) Question 7 (a)
  (e) Question 7 (b)
  (f) Question 7 (b)
  (g) Question 7 (a)

35. Selecting evidence for synthesis

1 For example: Byington says that **'I can't change what was, but I can help change what will be'.**
2 'Freedom or death': 'arouse enough feeling to bring about peace'; 'you cannot make omelettes without breaking eggs'; 'We were determined to press this question of the enfranchisement of women'; 'they couldn't wait any longer'.
'Wayward plastic': 'needs a meaningful response'; 'ways to compromise'; 'an important move'; 'I did the only thing I could think of'.
3 (a) Extract (ii)
  (b) Extract (i)

36. Synthesising evidence

1 consider, the role of women in society, both
2 For example:
'Freedom or death': 'women asked questions in political meetings and failed to get answers', 'first people who were put out of a political meeting for asking questions', 'We were called militant', 'you sacrificed the women'.
I am Malala: 'Don't wake up like me and realise what you missed', 'Getting an education is helping

her become more confident so that she can speak up outside', 'I was considered 'the smart girl''.
3 (a) 'Similarly', 'Both texts suggest', 'In both texts'
  (b) For example: For Malala, this is shown in her mother now being able to 'speak up outside' due to her education. Pankhurst also wants women to be able to speak up, in being able to start 'asking questions' in the same way as men without being 'brutally ill-used'.

37. Looking closely at language

1 'for no good reason' **suggests that the writer did not have a good reason for making his choice, it was a superficial judgement.**
'slicing rain' suggests that the rain is so fierce, that it feels as if it is cutting into the body.
'gleaming palaces of comfort' suggests that the hotels look so luxurious they could be fit for royalty.
2 For example: The notion that Bournemouth has little to offer is strengthened by the use of the adverb, 'only' suggesting that there is nothing else. The reference to 'gleaming palaces' suggests that the hotels look impressive and palatial, although it may be inferred that the 'gleaming' is a veneer.
3 (a) For example: The use of the simile, 'like a gopher' suggests **that the writer feels that the underground subways make him feel that he is a creature underground, coming up to find his location.**
  (b) The opening sentence is a multi-clause sentence and the writer uses it to convey the series of changes in the area around Bournemouth station. This creates the effect that so many changes have taken place that this causes confusion for the writer.

38. Planning to compare

1 Complete plan should include example quotations and explanation as detailed below for Extract 2. You should have examples for each from Extract 1 which will enable you to see the differences and any similarities as suggested in the 'Tone' section of the planning.
Tone:
- irritated, informal, frustrated, e.g. 'I'm gonna lose my mind', elements of colloquialisms, formal tone of Extract 1, e.g. standard English, no colloquialisms
Rhetorical devices/language
- negative view of spinners, supported with quotation from, e.g. school principal
- use of 'Twitter' to show the teacher's frustration and support schools' viewpoints
- provides examples of why fidget spinners are a problem, e.g. 'Kids are trading them'
Sentence structure:
- Long, multi-clause sentences to enable, e.g. principal to express her view on the reality of fidget spinners in schools and their negative effects.

39. Comparing ideas and perspectives

1 For example: Both texts start by expressing ideas about **family life and expectations of how we should live.**
2 For example: Unlike the father in *I am Malala*, Burville believes that children should **'develop a backbone'. This connotes that she thinks young people should be doing more for themselves and not relying on their parents. This clearly conflicts with the father getting breakfast every day for his children.**
3 For example:
Point: Both texts refer to family life and the extent to which teenagers are cared for.

121

Evidence: In Extract 1, the main focus is on adapting to a new life and the role of education: 'Here in the UK, teachers expect more from their students.' Burville's perspective is unchanged as she believes that there comes a point where teenagers should stop relying on their parents and 'accept some of the responsibility'. Explanation: In a sense, both extracts consider expectations of students, but for Malala the focus is on responding to the different academic demands in a different school.

40. Answering a comparison question

1 Answers should:
  - compare the language and structure of the two texts
  - focus on the effect of the writers' language and structural choices
  - support key points with evidence and explanation/analysis.

Examples of points you could make in your paragraph:
  - Both texts use emotive language to engage the reader from the opening paragraph – Text 1 uses 'shot by the Taliban' and Text 2 talks about 'going viral'. They are attempting to draw in the reader.
  - Both texts are about the struggle of being a teenager and both texts use humour. However, the writer of Text 1 is describing a very serious and emotional situation which means we get a positive idea of her as a teenager. In Text 2, teenagers are talked about in a negative light.
  - Text 2 poses a question followed by the answer (hypophora), 'But is it a new problem? The answer is no, and the solution isn't new either.' Hinting at a possible solution to be actioned engages the reader. In contrast, the writer of Text 1 is talking about the actions she has already taken, and the reader is inspired to be like her so the reader is engaged in a different way.
  - Both writers use exclamation marks which emphasises the link in the extracts to teenagers and youth.
  - Yousafza uses pattern of three to describe the daily struggle her mother has with normal situations, 'gone shopping, or to the doctor, or the bank'. Similarly, Burville uses lists to show the wide variety of jobs teenagers obviously struggle to complete, '*Rake the leaves, mow the lawn, shovel the walk…*'. The effect is similar as both writers are emphasising how much needs to be done.

41. Putting it into practice

1 Answers could include the following key points (but remember to **compare** each point in Text 1 with a corresponding point in Text 2):
  'Guidance from the Past'
  - direct address to reader as opening: 'I'm sure you've heard' as a way to engage reader from the beginning
  - has modern contexts with references to media shares which links with youth culture
  - uses bracketed comments for humorous aside '(unless the parents were paying)'.
  - presents text in context and gives key dates
  - gives more detail from original text with contemporary comment from the writer, 'Opinions are divided on this old-school advice.'
  - text ends with update of information about context/source.
  I am Malala
  - begins with background of arriving in England and refers to upheaval using verbs such as 'plucked' and 'transported'

  - shows admiration and surprise at father doing the catering – use of adverb 'jokingly' suggests comfortable relationship between father and daughter
  - considers significance of education not only from teenage viewpoint but also how it helps the mother – 'biggest changes of all… so that she can speak up outside the home, not just inside with us' (contrasts with perception of 'selfish ego' in 'Guidance from the Past')
  - describes forming and maintaining friendships (teenage friendships not explored in other text)
  - appreciates education as a means for progression/advancement 'helping their communities'.

42. Evaluating a text

1 Read the question, Read the text, Annotate key quotations, Plan your answer, Write your answer
2 Ideas: What the writer thinks or believes
  Events: What happens or is described
  Themes: Think about a text's tone or purpose
  Settings: Where and when things happen
3

Paper 1, Question 4	Paper 2, Question 6
How long to spend on answer: **30 mins**	How long to spend on answer: **15 mins**
Focus of question: **narrator as imaginative story-teller**	Focus of question: **engaging descriptions of his experience**
I'll need to look at **an effect that is created in the extract**	I'll need to look at **one specific aspect of the extract**

43. Evaluating a text: fiction

1 For example:
  'grew bitter' – continuing bad feeling and his presence actually changed Hindley
  'changed my ideas' – Heathcliff changes people
  'Heathcliff as a usurper' 'privileges' – Heathcliff disrupts the established order of inheritance
  'affections' – Heathcliff even affects fondness/good feelings
  'death' – associated with death/tragedy
2 For example: The setting successfully creates a negative impression of Heathcliff, as in the opening line his influence on the house is described as breeding 'bad feeling' which **is 'from the very beginning', emphasising how powerful and negative an impact was made. The author successfully creates the impression that Heathcliff is a strong presence and provokes formidable reactions. It appears that he is not a character who can be regarded neutrally. He elicits long-term resentment from Hindley but manages to gain an ally in the narrator.**
3 Events could include:
  (a) he chooses the more handsome horse – shows favouritism/taking Hindley's right
  (b) he gains possession of Hindley's horse when his goes lame – using blackmail/deceit
  (c) the confrontation in the stable when Hindley attacks him – prompts physical violence.
4 For example: The writer presents Heathcliff as 'uncomplaining' when he was ill, but it is suggested that this is because he is unfeeling rather than gentle. The writer's description of Heathcliff's 'hardness' when he is ill gives the reader an insight into his true character. He gains an 'ally' in Miss Dean but does not appear to

interact with others, being described as 'insensible'. It is inferred that Heathcliff had first choice of the horse but when his went lame he did not hesitate to go after Hindley's horse: 'You must.' He uses blackmail to get what he wants, threatening Hindley with 'I shall tell' and leading Hindley to be physically punished, 'you'll get them again with interest'. The writer is effective in building up an atmosphere of violence by beginning with dialogue and threats and ending with physical harm. Although he is knocked down by the weight and clearly in pain, 'breathless and white', he does not let that defeat him, getting up 'immediately'. The writer is successful in presenting Heathcliff as a determined character who will not let something like physical pain stop him from getting what he wants.

44. Evaluating a text: non-fiction

1 For example: 'when they felt they couldn't wait any longer', 'obstinate British government' suggests that 'they' wanted action, but 'obstinate' suggests they are not meeting co-operation
   'absolutely disregarded' – what they wanted was totally ignored so had to act
   'every other means had failed' – no choice
   'they went on until they had won' – actions got results

2 For example: 'a good many women had to go without their tea' – loss of tea might not be top priority but draws on the humorous cliché that a cup of tea is an essential in life

3 For example:
   • uses historical context to present the idea for action – 'your forefathers decided'
   • reminds them they too wanted 'representation'
   • repetition: 'many, many' for emphasis
   • 'laid all their arguments' suggests preparation and sense of righteousness
   • uses language which presents British negatively: 'obstinate', 'absolutely disregarded'
   • presents Americans positively – 'when every other means failed'.

4 For example: The writer successfully uses the historical context of American independence as a vehicle to justify the actions of women in Britain as they campaign for the vote. She uses the structure of the events with her own commentary on why they had to have the 'tea party.' She uses positive terms to describe the Americans: 'decided they wanted', 'laid all their arguments' and 'when every other means failed' to present them as trying everything before they had to take action. This makes her sound reasonable and is effective in persuading the reader. She presents the British as 'obstinate' and unsympathetic to a cause which they 'absolutely disregarded'.

45. Putting it into practice

1 Answers could include the following key points:
   • Fred discussed by others outside the context of this extract – others disapprove of his attitude and it is worth talking about
   • Fred's future (taking orders means becoming a vicar) – should he become a clergyman because it is expected/others have invested in him?
   • the dialogue created by the writer is realistic: the discussion between Mary and Rosamond is structured to change in tone and direction which is effective in building up the conflicting opinions of the characters

   • Mary and Rosamond conflict because Mary does not think Fred should do as required as that would make him 'a hypocrite'
   • the writer is successful in maintaining the tension between the different characters: Mary and Rosamond argue until the end of the extract – can't agree
   • the writer challenges expectations when Mary says you should do a role suitable for you – 'violent' disagreement with expectations
   • however, the writer balances this when Rosamond says you should become suitable for the role designated to you – 'mild' acceptance
   • conflict between self-determination and duty
   • the writer uses the culture of gentility as a backdrop to the conversation: 'horrid' as an unsuitable word for the characters' status
   • Mary defends Fred because he also supports her – does not mean she necessarily agrees
   • Rosamond sympathises with her father – as she would be expected to do as his daughter
   • Look also at sentence structure as covered earlier in the revision workbook.

46. Putting it into practice

1 Answers could include the following key points:
   • ideas: the main being adaptation to life in England/homesickness
   • first paragraph: the writer gives reader sense of context and time 'a year', 'two years' – gives reader temporal references but also suggests that much has changed for the family in a very short space of time
   • the writer provokes a sense of surprise by the use of language: 'plucked', 'transported' and 'pinch myself' idiom to show her disbelief – this is done very effectively as it ensures the reader feels empathy with the writer
   • the writer uses contrast to describe the immediate impact on family: father who caters 'astonishing' and contrasts with life in Swat where he didn't 'even know the price of a pint of milk' – now 'knows where everything is on the shelves'. Writer's use of contrast is effective in adding a lighter tone to the text
   • power of education: mother is learning literacy skills and English, which will give her freedom and her own voice 'outside the home'
   • theme: adjusting to life – the writer is effective in using environments and situations that are very familiar to the reader but that are unfamiliar to her family which is engaging for the reader
   • contrasts of valley in Swat with life in 'second-biggest city'
   • mother without the language is now going to classes
   • the climate 'constant rain' 'to me that feels like spring'
   • education system: they 'expect more from their students.

SECTION B: WRITING

47. Writing questions: an overview

1 (a) Paper 1   (c) Paper 2   (e) Both
   (b) Paper 2   (d) Both

2 (a) AO6   (c) AO6   (e) AO5
   (b) AO6   (d) AO5

3 For example: Assessment objective 5(a): write fluently and engagingly, using appropriate techniques according to audiences, purposes and styles.

Assessment objective 5(b): Arrange **ideas effectively, using appropriate techniques to ensure text is clear**.
Assessment objective 6: Use wide selection of words in a range of sentence styles and use accurate spelling and punctuation throughout.

48. Writing questions: Paper 1

1 (a) Answer provided on page 48
   (b) True
   (c) True
   (d) True
2 This phrase should be circled: 'Your response could be real or imagined.'
3 'may' means that using the images is optional
4 (a) Answer provided on page 48
   (b) Planning your answer: 10 minutes
   (c) Writing your answer: 30 minutes
   (d) Checking and proofreading your answer: 5 minutes

49. Writing questions: Paper 2

1 Transactional writing is usually:
   • Answer provided on page 49
   • intended to achieve a specific purpose/~~amusing and light-hearted~~
   • ~~entertaining and humorous~~/serious, with humour only if appropriate to the audience
   • for a specific audience/~~suitable for all ages~~
   • Answer provided on page 49
2 (a) Question 8 – school magazine, Question 9 – website as information for other visitors
   (b) Question 8 – article, Question 9 – review
   (c) Question 8 – suggesting ways that the pressures of work could be reduced, Question 9 – as information for other visitors
3

Planning your answer	Answer provided on page 49
Writing your answer	11.10–11.40 am
Checking and proofreading your answer	11.40–11.45 am

50. Writing for a purpose: imaginative

1 For example:

see:	The rain clouds gathering
hear:	Answer provided on page 50
smell:	The scent of pine needles
touch:	The strap of my school bag
taste:	The moisture in the air

2 For example: There was a soft rustling in the hedge.
3 For example: I was very curious about what was making the noise, it was **something I had not heard before and it was getting louder, almost desperate. I was beginning to get worried.**
4 For example: Simile: It sounded like **a gaggle of angry geese**.
   Metaphor: The clouds were brooding cliffs in the sky.
   Personification: The undergrowth moaned and muttered with increasing panic.
5 Answers should:
   • use the senses
   • include examples of figurative language
   • include examples of carefully chosen language
   • use verbs that show rather than tell
   • maintain one narrative voice throughout.

For example: I was very curious about what was making the noise, it was something I had not heard before and it was getting louder, almost desperate. I was beginning to get worried. It sounded like a herd of angry elephants, a stampede even, but all in one place, buried in the undergrowth, which moaned and muttered with increasing panic. The scent of the pine needles grew ever stronger, as with a grasp of the strap of my school bag, I took a deep breath and headed towards the commotion.

51. Writing for a purpose: inform, explain, review

1 An informative tone that could be casual and humorous.
2 Example subheadings could include:
   (a) About the school
   (b) Local attractions
   (c) Places to go outside the area
   (d) Answer provided on page 51
3 (a) This fact will not fit the needed upbeat tone of the piece.
   (b) This fact is not relevant.
   (c) This fact is clearly untrue.
4 Answers might include subheadings and should include examples of facts and statistics. The tone should be formal. For example:
   The school is a major resource in the community. It is a built-for-purpose centre for learning, in its own grounds with fantastic indoor and outdoor sports facilities, as well as an outstanding performing arts centre. Over 70% of students use the school leisure facilities at the weekend and it is open to the local community both at the weekends and in the evenings.

52. Writing for a purpose: argue and persuade

1 Examples of points that **disagree** with the idea could include: the park is the only green area for miles around, there is plenty of land that could be used such as where the abandoned warehouses are located, it is well used by the community and outside visitors. Examples of points that **agree** with the idea could include: the park has become overgrown and a community eyesore, there are other places to create parkland, the park and nature reserve are hardly visited.
2 Answers will vary. Remember, you can make up evidence, so long as it is believable. For example:
   Agree – park has become overgrown and a community eyesore.
   Evidence – complaints from locals about how it is not being maintained and encourages anti-social behaviour.
   Disagree – there is plenty of land that can be used such as where the abandoned warehouses are located.
   Evidence – the land belongs to the council, there are many acres which would hold many homes.
3 For example:
   Agree – Some people might feel **that the nature reserve is so poorly maintained that we cannot get in there anyway.** However, **with support from our proactive community groups and some organisation, this is a problem with a solution.**
   Disagree – Some people might feel **that we are short of open spaces in the local community and that this decision would contradict the council's pledge to promote healthy lifestyles.** However, **there are other areas which can be made into parkland, and we do have outdoor gyms and other community outdoor spaces.**

4 For example:

    (a) Alliteration: This is a <u>d</u>espicable and <u>d</u>ubious decision.

    (b) Pattern of three: The park is used by <u>children</u>, <u>adults</u> and <u>communities</u> alike.

    (c) Rhetorical question: <u>Where will these go if the park closes?</u>

53. Writing for an audience

1 For example: The audience is likely to be **over 25 and both genders; younger people may read it because of their use of social media**.

2 For example: With the increasing use of social media, there is a risk that people will forget how to just talk to each other face to face.

3 Answers should be appropriate for an adult audience, so language should be formal. At any time, non-standard English, slang and texting language should be avoided. A variety of sentence structures and a wide vocabulary should be used. For example:

There has been a lot of discussion in our year about whether or not we should still wear school uniform. A strong argument for keeping school uniform is linked with the cost of designer wear and how some students would find it difficult to keep up with their more wealthy peers. **Removing the school uniform would be culturally and economically divisive, threatening a sense of community and posing a distraction to learning. It would be a retrograde step.**

54. Putting it into practice

1 (a) Answer provided on page 54

    (b) Planning time: 10 minutes

    (c) Writing time: 30 minutes

    (d) Checking time: 5 minutes

    (e) Form: prose

    (f) Narrative voice: not specified

2 Examples of language will vary, but might include: using the senses, figurative language, contrast, direct address.

3 For example:

    (a) Contrast – As he looked down the great drop, he felt as small as the cliff face was massive.

    (b) Direct address – She didn't want to go in. Would you have done it?

55. Putting it into practice

1 For example:

	Question 8
Timing	Plan: 10 minutes Write: 30 minutes Check: 5 minutes
Topic	New cinema complex
Form	Review
Audience	Teenagers
Purpose	To inform

	Question 9
Timing	Plan: 10 minutes Write: 30 minutes Check: 5 minutes
Topic	Gaming is waste of time
Form	Article
Audience	School students
Purpose	To argue and persuade

56. Form: articles and reviews

1 For example: Headline (**c**) is the best because **it is interesting, formal and sums up the article topic.**

2 Answers will vary but, again, must be suitable for an adult audience. For example: Can we put a price on experience?

3 Answers will vary but, again, must be suitable for an adult audience. For example:

    (a) Answer provided on page 56

    (b) Source provided on page 56. **Fact:** 40% of students who felt pressured to go to university dropped out within a year.

4 Answers should include figurative devices or language techniques matched to annotated words in the question. For example:

Local: as important to the town as the Eiffel tower in Paris

Full upgrade: every inch is brand new and begging to be explored

New rides: the park's biggest rollercoaster is a gigantic python winding around the park

57. Form: letters and reports

1

Informal language	Incorrect use of word	Incorrect punctuation
reckon tons old grumpies hang around	stuck additionally Yours sincerely	you know what.

2 For example: It was undoubtedly the school's positive welcome, the entertaining organised trips and the touching farewell ceremony that made this visit so successful.

3 For example:

    (a) One possible project could be **a joint activities weekend for Year 11 students from both schools. This would enable both sets of students to interact in an out of school environment, responding to challenges and enhancing life skills.**

    (b) **I would also suggest an arts week for both schools, hosted here or at our visitors' school, where we can showcase our talents in a 'fringe festival' context.**

58. Form: information guides

1 For example:

    (a) Answer provided on page 58

    (b) A lesson learned

    (c) Lessons, learning, leisure

2 For example: 'Lessons, learning, leisure' would be the most effective because it suggests to the reader that the school is a positive experience and involves leisure as well as learning.

3 For example:

    (a) Answer provided on page 58

    (b) Where's the fun?

    (c) After school hours

4 For example:

    • typical school day

    • school fun days

    • clubs and after-school activities

5 For example: No two school days are exactly the same at this school – because that depends on your lesson and classes. However, there are a few important events that are at the same time every day.

Answers to 1, 3, 4 and 5 should use language appropriate for secondary school students and may use some informal language, although Standard English must always be used.

59. Putting it into practice

1 Answers should be suitable for an adult audience and written in a formal style. They will include features of a letter:
   - Dear …
   - A subject line
   - Key points
   - Evidence, e.g. facts and/or statistics
   - Counter-arguments
   - Rhetorical devices to signpost a path through points made
   - A conclusion
   - Yours …

60. Prose: an overview

1 Prose because this is what is specified by the exam board

2 (c) poems should be ticked

3 For example: Prose is continuous **writing, using sentences and paragraphs.**

4 Narrative: Extract B
   Description: Extract A
   Monologue: Extract C

61. Ideas and planning: imaginative

1 Either of the two questions could be chosen.

2 Answers will vary, depending on the question chosen in Question 1, but should answer key questions about the **characters**: e.g. who is there? Personality/appearance? And the **action**: e.g. what is happening and what has happened already?

3 Details added should develop ideas and include examples of figurative devices and use of the senses, For example, for Question 6: 'The road was in continuous curves (alliteration) like a snake (simile)'.

62. Structure: imaginative

1 Answers will vary but all should:
   - complete the narrative structure with a balanced amount of detail for each stage
   - include ideas about imaginative writing techniques.
   For example:
   Exposition: At first appears a genuinely nice person, always cheerful and **willing to help anybody with anything**.
   Rising action: **During an outdoor pursuits weekend he encourages someone in the group to cross a rope bridge. The person is scared, very brief reference, show fear in dialogue, he reassures character that bridge is safe.**
   Climax: **Bridge collapses, person falls in water, covered in mud and distressed – show through description of reaction and mud, he laughs, admits (dialogue) knew bridge might collapse, films it all on mobile.**
   Falling action: **Threatens to post film on social media, describe gestures, body language.**
   Resolution: **Someone deletes film, he is no longer in friendship group, person who fell from bridge supported by friends – describe how we know this – show not tell, adjectives, adverbs.**

2 Answers should adapt Question 1, using flashback structure.
   For example:
   Climax: Bridge collapses, person falls in water, covered in mud and distressed – show through description of reaction and mud, he laughs, admits (dialogue) knew bridge might collapse, films it all on mobile.
   Exposition: At first appears a genuinely nice person, always cheerful and willing to help anybody with anything.

Rising action: During an outdoor pursuits' weekend he encourages someone in the group to cross a rope bridge. The person is scared, very brief reference, show fear in dialogue, he reassures character that bridge is safe.
Return to climax – What happens at the bridge.
Falling action: Threatens to post film on social media, describe gestures, body language.
Resolution: Someone deletes film, he is no longer in friendship group, person who fell from bridge supported by friends – describe how we know this – show not tell, adjectives, adverbs.

63. Beginnings and endings: imaginative

1 Responses will vary. For example:
   One-sentence description: **My best friend and I forgot our swimming costumes**.
   Narrative voice: **first person**
   Who is involved: **me, teacher and best friend**
   Where is the story set: **swimming pool lockers**

2 Dialogue: **'Brrrrr. Aren't you getting ready then?' 'I will in a minute,' I replied, 'I just need to take my shoes off first.'**
   I put off admitting the embarrassing truth for as long as I could: I had forgotten my swimming costume.
   Experience/context: **There is a running joke that whoever forgets to bring in their swimming costume will have to wear the brown frilly one that is always hanging up in the locker room. I always thought it was a funny joke: maybe because I never thought I would be that person.**
   Conflict: **I laughed at my best friend's face as he realised his swimming costume wasn't in his bag. But my joy quickly turned to horror as I realised that mine wasn't either.**

3 Answers will vary depending on Question 1. For example: And it goes without saying that we never forgot our swimming costumes again!

4 For example:
   (a) Looking back, it was the making of us, although there must be easier ways to gain essential life skills!
   (b) As experiences go, it was definitely memorable but not necessarily for all the right reasons.
   (c) We are grateful for what we gained from the experience, and certainly grateful that it is now in the past!

64. Putting it into practice

1 Plans should include:
   - some form of five-part narrative structure, for example a spider diagram or numbered points for sequencing
   - ideas for beginning and ending
   - details of narrative voice and imaginative writing techniques to be used.

65. Ideas and planning: inform, explain, review

1 Plans should include:
   - a title
   - an introduction and a conclusion
   - ideas for subheadings, if appropriate
   - an opening paragraph
   - three or four sequenced key points (numbered in a logical way)
   - a range of supporting details.

66. Ideas and planning: argue and persuade

1 For example:
   (a) Phones should not be banned because they are needed for emergencies, organising lifts and social reasons.

(b) The people who want mobile phones banned are the people who won't even be affected by it: this cannot be allowed to happen, as any student would tell you.

(c) Point 1: Answer provided on page 66
Evidence: Answer provided on page 66
Point 2: **Students can look up problems on phones, saving teachers time.**
Evidence: **Many learning apps have been created for this reason.**
Point 3: **Students focus better knowing they are not missing out on anything socially.**
Evidence: **Professor Fallon of Warwick University did a study that showed students without their phones found it harder to concentrate in lessons.**

(d) Responses will vary but points should be numbered in a logical sequence.

(e) Some people might claim that teachers should be teaching and not using technology, but it means teachers have more time for those who need direct help.

(f) Banning phones would not only impact on students' rights, social lives, happiness and safety, but also on their ability to learn at school.

67. Openings: transactional

1 Answers will vary. For example: The rhetorical question because it makes the reader think how they would react if censorship happened to them.

2 ~~In this article, I am going to argue that~~ internet access should not be controlled for under 18-year-olds. Would you feel comfortable talking to friends, going to work or even watching TV knowing that someone else was controlling what you did?

68. Conclusions: transactional

1 For example:
End on a vivid image: Answer provided on page 68
End on a warning: **If we don't start respecting animals and their right to exist in their natural habitat, many more will become extinct.**
End on a happy note: **We are far more aware of animal welfare than ever before and more and more is being achieved to restore habitats and release animals into the wild.**
End on a thought-provoking question: **If we don't take responsibility for animals, what will become of them in the future?**
End on a 'call to action': **It is time to take a stand and we can start by not visiting places where animals are used for entertainment.**

2 Answers will vary but should include a suitable explanation for why the technique chosen would be most effective.

69. Putting it into practice

1 Plans should include:
- an engaging title
- a subheading
- an idea for an engaging opening paragraph
- ideas for three sequenced paragraphs with details of figurative language/language devices to be used
- an idea for a conclusion.

70. Paragraphing for effect

1 Point: Many of us appreciate that music, art and drama enrich our lives but **how these subjects could be included in our current, over-crowded curriculum is a major issue**.

Evidence: **We have full timetables now.**
Explain: **So, short of extending the school day, the arts could only be included at the expense of other subjects.**

2 (a) point
(b) explanation
(c) Answer provided on page 70
(d) explanation
(e) point
(f) explanation
(g) evidence

3 For example: Arts subjects are more difficult to make a career from so shouldn't be compulsory. This is shown by only 5% of universities asking for an arts qualification for their courses, showing that the other subjects are more important and so deserve more time.

4 The paragraph should be labelled to show the point, evidence and explanation.

71. Linking ideas

1 Adding an idea: **Furthermore, Moreover**
Explaining: **Consequently, Therefore**
Illustrating: For example, **For instance**
Emphasising: **In particular, Significantly**
Comparing: **In the same way, Similarly**
Contrasting: **However, On the other hand**

2 Paragraph 1: for instance, therefore
Paragraph 2: moreover, furthermore

3 Answers will vary, but should use the P–E–E structure and feature a range of adverbials. For example: In particular, if the school imposes the ban, this may have a significant impact on families struggling with low incomes. 'Healthy' foods are often more expensive. On the other hand, schools have a duty of care during the school day and nutritious food is often linked to more effective learning.

72. Putting it into practice

1 Answers should include:
- appropriate features for audience, purpose and form
- well-structured and sequenced paragraphs, with one main idea or main point per paragraph
- a range of adverbials to link paragraphs and guide the reader.

73. Vocabulary for effect: synonyms

1 For example:
Extra: more, additional
Classes: lessons, programmes
Significant: substantial, major
Outcomes: results, marks

2 For example:
angry: annoyed, enraged, vexed
happy: glad, pleased, joyful
shout: yell, bellow, roar
anxious: Answers provided on page 73.
confident: poised, assured, self-reliant

3 Answers will vary, but should include some of the synonyms from Question 2. For example: On that fateful day, I knew I had enraged him. I was apprehensive as I tried to explain my actions, but he was more than a little annoyed. His voice was a bellow and a roar, with nothing less frightening in between.

4 Answers will vary, but should include the information from Question 3 presented in an uninteresting way. For example: I knew I made him angry on that day. I explained my actions, but he was annoyed. He shouted and it was scary.

74. Vocabulary for effect: argue and persuade

1 (a) excessive, disastrous
   (b) drastic, serious
   (c) horrible, cruelly

2 For example:
   (a) Some parents are <u>furious</u> about the school's <u>ridiculous</u> plan to ban unhealthy food from the school's premises.
   (b) Some <u>livid</u> parents are <u>outraged</u> about the <u>tyrannical</u> school's <u>disastrous</u> plan to ban unhealthy food from the school's premises.
   (c) Some parents are <u>extremely</u> unhappy about the school's <u>outrageous scheme</u> to ban unhealthy food from the school's premises.

3 Answers will vary, but should consist of two sentences and include vocabulary chosen for its impact and connotations. For example: The increasing incidents of litter and vandalism are threatening to our sense of well-being and detrimental to our way of life. This situation has become uncontrollable and must be addressed by the council and the police as a matter of desperate urgency.

75. Language for different effects 1

1 For example:
   Contrast: Outside the doors of the deserted sweetshop, the town square was heaving with enthusiastic shoppers.
   Repetition: The only thing busier than the town square was how busy the people were as they bustled about on their busy business.
   Rhetorical question: Answer provided on page 75
   List: Parents, children, grandparents, uncles, aunts – it seemed everyone was there that day.

2 Answers will vary. For example: The list because it shows just how many people there were.

3 Answers will vary. For example: List: I have always taken an interest in animal welfare, often helping neighbours by walking the dog, feeding animals when the owners were away and cleaning cages and hutches. Not only do I have this experience, but I am also enthusiastic, caring, helpful and always very punctual.

76. Language for different effects 2

1 A Hyperbole
   B Direct address
   C Alliteration
   D Pattern of three
   E Direct address
   F Answer provided on page 76

2 Answers will vary. For example: Alliteration because the sound mimics the way the student is moving.

3 Answers will vary, but should use one or more of the language techniques explored in Question 1.
   For example:
   Direct address: You must be wondering why we have a new dining block and social area, when we had one already.
   Hyperbole: I expect there are thousands of good reasons for this project, but I can't think of one that is even remotely justifiable.
   Pattern of three: The great day came, the crowds gathered and the block was officially opened.
   Alliteration: Purposefully, people powered forward to admire the state-of-the-art-building.

77. Language for different effects 3

1 For example:
   (a) Answer provided on page 77
   (b) Learning anything is like trying to climb up a soapy, slippery slope.
   (c) The moon was like a white cat creeping into every garden.
   (d) The exam paper is a locked box and we can only guess what is inside.
   (e) The staircase taunted us, laughing and saying we would never reach its top.
   (f) She was a snake, moving on silent scales.

2 Answers will vary, but should be in the form of four extracts and use one or more of the language techniques explored in Question 1. For example:
   Simile: The secrecy was like a lead weight, dragging me down with its burden.
   Metaphor: The secret had me locked in my own prison.
   Simile: Whenever I felt tempted to speak of it, it was as if there was an invisible gag, silencing me.
   Personification: The terror kept pace with me: shoulder to shoulder.

78. Using the senses

1 Any of the choices could be circled as it is according to personal choice.

2 Answers will vary according to the extracts circled in Question 1, but the explanation should reflect the 'show not tell' technique of using the senses.

3 Answers will vary, but the explanation should include why the example is effective due to the 'show not tell' technique.

4 Answers will vary, but all should:
   • consist of one paragraph
   • use a sense other than sight and the 'show not tell' technique
   • include examples of figurative language such as simile, metaphor and personification.
   For example: He had no idea how he had got there. This was a strange, desolate place and he broke into a sweat when he realised he was not alone. There, on the horizon, a mountainous mass was moving towards him, the shrill shrieks pierced the air and echoed around him. **The air was thick with a smell like rotting eggs, wrapping its putrid arms around my face and nose, making my eyes water.**

79. Narrative voice

1 For example: He knew he was supposed to be disappointed and that everyone thought he was 'putting a brave face on it'. The truth? He was so relieved, they had no idea!

2 Answers will vary but should consist of two possible openings. Each opening should:
   • consist of one or two sentences
   • use a different narrative voice.
   For example:
   (a) I approached along the path warily, **knowing that I should not be in the grounds, much less intending to enter the house itself**.
   (b) He could sense that something was hiding in the upstairs of the house, so the house was not abandoned in the usual sense. Despite this, he continued towards the door; he had given his word that he would do this.

80. Putting it into practice

1 Answers should include examples of:
- language appropriate to form, purpose and audience
- language chosen for effect
- figurative devices
- language techniques, e.g. rhetorical questions, pattern of three.

81. Putting it into practice

1 Answers should include:
- language appropriate to audience
- ambitious and effective language choices
- a range of language techniques, including figurative devices
- a consistent narrative voice.

82. Sentence variety 1

1 (a) After she ate, she read her book.
(b) She read her book and she ate grapes.
(c) She read her book, which she had bought.
(d) Answer provided on page 82

2 For example: Celebrities often complain that they do not have enough privacy, stating that they are photographed all the time. They also complain that the pictures are edited to reflect them in a poor light, so the pictures are cropped to present a particular image of the celebrity. They don't, however, complain at fees paid by celebrity magazines, and they want publicity for their films. They can't have it both ways. Choose!

83. Sentence variety 2

1 An adverb
2 For example:
(a) Answer provided on page 83
(b) Frustrated, I had to ask for help as I couldn't sort out the problem on my own.
(c) However, I managed to make everything better eventually.
3 Answers will vary, but should aim to:
- include at least four different types of sentence opener from Question 2
- use a different word to start each sentence.
For example:
His behaviour appeared strange immediately and we realised he was someone to avoid if we could. **The** people near him were distancing themselves from his behaviour. **Behind** him, a crowd was watching from a safe distance. **Hurrying**, we moved to go **around** him and away. **Aggressive**, threatening and menacing from the outset, he barred our way. **Carefully**, we approached him. **He** still seemed fierce, **although** he was calm once he had the 'doggy treats', and his grateful owner had him safely on his leash.

84. Sentences for different effects

1 For example: The effect of the multi-clause sentence is to link all the sequences of events together. The effect of the minor sentence is to emphasise the extent of the catastrophe.

2 For example: Alarmingly, he would be back soon. Between his arrival and my explanations, I needed a miracle to happen. I assessed the full extent of the damage. All the paperwork and books were saturated and no amount of drying them would help. Hurrying to mop up the water, I tried hard to make it look less of a wreck.

3 For example: The order in which the information is organised can determine whether the emphasis is on the narrator's need to clear up the mess or the alarming prospect of 'his' unwelcome return.

4 Answers will vary but all should aim to include:
- a long, multi-clause sentence, followed by a short, single-clause sentence
- a sentence structured to give specific emphasis.
For example: Our annual fund-raising event had all the usual attention that reflects its high-profile status in the local community: local newspapers, the mayor and the local news channels were all there. It became evident early in the day that this would be bigger than ever before. Vast crowds had gathered early.

85. Putting it into practice

1 Answers should include examples of:
- a range of sentence types
- sentences beginning in a range of different ways
- sentences structured for effect.

86. Ending a sentence

1 A Correct
B Incorrect. 'Since' should be lowercase.
C Incorrect. 'billy' should have a capital B.
D Correct
E Answer provided on page 86
2 (a) Full stop
(b) Question mark
(c) Full stop
(d) Question mark
(e) Exclamation mark
3 For example:
(a) Answer provided on page 86
(b) For example: Should I follow the path left or right?
(c) 'I never said you should jump in head first!'
4 Sentence A: Incorrect as this is a comma splice where either a conjunction is needed or two sentences.
Sentence B: Correct as the two sentences are joined with a conjunction: *but*.
Sentence C: Correct as the two sentences are separated with a full stop.
5 The stand-off
I have no intention of giving in this time. **(1)** He might think he will get away with it, but I am ready for him now. He will ask for money again, **(2)** with the promise of repaying me next week, but he has never repaid any money I have lent him. **(3)** It is time for me to make a stand! **(4)** How many more times will he ask me? **(5)** How long before he is able to get control of his finances? **(6)** I say this all stops now.

87. Commas

1 **Commas in lists**
A Correct
B Answer provided on page 87; there should not be a comma after 'when.'
C Correct
Commas in multi-clause sentences with subordinate clauses
D Incorrect. The main clause has come before the dependent clause in the example so there should be no comma. You could use a comma if the clauses were reversed. For example it would be correct to say: 'Even though some can be hard work, friends are very important.'
E Incorrect – should be a comma after 'time' and before 'we'.

129

F Correct

Commas in multi-clause sentences with relative clauses.

G Correct

H Incorrect – there should be a comma after 'someone' or no commas at all.

I Incorrect – there should also be a comma after 'once'.

2 For example:

(a) She was warm, friendly, funny and wise.

(b) Endlessly, we would share with her our hopes and dreams, which were always more impressive than anyone else's.

(c) To this day, and this is over many years, I have yet to meet anyone who would say otherwise.

88. Apostrophes and speech punctuation

1 and 2

Apostrophes in contractions

A Correct

B Incorrect – should be **It's**.

C Incorrect – should be **hasn't**.

Apostrophes of possession

D Answer provided on page 88

E Correct

F Incorrect – should be **group's**.

Speech punctuation

G Incorrect – should be **'Look out!'**

H Correct

I Incorrect – should be **that,** (not a full stop).

3 Answers will vary but should aim to use apostrophes and speech marks correctly. For example:

'Hey,' she called. 'You'll never guess what happened in History today.'

'What's that?' I asked. 'I didn't go because my dad's car broke down. Its engine wouldn't start.'

'Billy dropped Stacey's pencil case into Miss's fish tank. It landed on top of the fish's castle. I don't know if it's still in there because I'm too scared to check.'

'Was Miss mad?' I asked. 'I would've been and I heard she's well scary when she's mad.'

'She was really scary. Weren't you there when **Ami put up her hand and told the teacher that she was wrong? You should've seen Miss's face then!'**

'And was she – wrong that is?'

'I don't know,' she replied. 'We were too busy watching for what would happen next.'

89. Colons, semi-colons, dashes, brackets and ellipses

1 Dashes - or – This can be used singularly or in pairs to add extra information to a sentence.

Ellipses … This suggests missing information or a dramatic pause.

Brackets ( ) These are used in pairs to add extra information.

Semi-colons ; You can use this to link two connected ideas.

Colons : This introduces an example, list or explanation.

2 **A**: Answer provided on page 89

B: A healthy diet is vital; it can allow you to gain an edge over competitors who don't take care of their bodies.

C: Learning to be a good loser is essential; everybody tastes defeat at some point.

D: I have always been good at the flute (since I can remember anyway) but wanted to be better.

E: Some cyclists take to the road without wearing a safety helmet: not a good idea.

3 Answers will vary but all should aim to use:

- a colon and semi-colon
- dashes, brackets and ellipsis (…).

For example: The cat was vicious: hissing and scratching. I still helped it; I couldn't leave it (even if I was terrified). I put some food in the cat cage and waited … slowly – and very carefully – it went inside.

90. Putting it into practice

1 Answers should feature a range of punctuation used accurately, including advanced punctuation such as colons and semi-colons.

91. Common spelling errors 1

1 (a) **Their** books were soaked and covered in wet grass.

(b) The dog lifted **its** injured paw.

(c) We are all **affected** by people's moods.

(d) The abandoned shed is over **there**.

(e) We **could have** finished that if we hadn't given up.

(f) **Are** you ready yet? We don't want to miss the bus.

(g) When people are cheerful, we respond **positively**.

(h) You **should have** thought of that before we left the house.

92. Common spelling errors 2

1 (a) Answer provided on page 92

(b) They **were** so lucky that the weather was good for the race.

(c) I enjoy learning about **past** events in history.

(d) I thought there were three bottles of water, but there are only **two**.

(e) You obviously got caught in the rain as **you're** soaked!

2 (a) He climbed to the top **of** the hill.

(b) We need to clear the room. **Whose** jacket is on the chair?

(c) The weather is so unpredictable; it is hard to decide what to **wear**.

(d) She was so pleased when she **passed** her exams with good grades.

(e) He wanted **to** go to the beach but everyone thought it was too cold.

93. Common spelling errors 3

1 Correct spellings:

Difficult

Occasionally

Embarrassing

Beginning

Recommend

Separately

Definitely

Argument

Experience

Disappoint

Disappear

Conscious

Conscience

Believe

Possession

Independence

Business

Rhythm

Decision

Weird

Grateful

2 Answers will vary.

94. Proofreading

1 The corrections needed in the extract are shown in bold. As usual, we **were** waiting for the bus by the entrance **to** the national park. It was some time before we realised what was going on. **There** was the noise of something crashing about in the undergrowth and then little cries of distress. We are not the bravest people in the world, but the **bus wasn't** due for ages and there **were** others out and about if we needed help.

Advancing cautiously, we crept into the undergrowth and **there,** trapped in the branches of a low-hanging tree, was a very young beautiful baby deer. It wasn't **afraid** of us; it kept still as we **freed** it. Then it scampered away, no harm done!

2 and **3** Answers will vary depending on the work chosen. Spelling practised will vary depending on the errors found for Question 2.

95. Putting it into practice

1 Answers should feature accurately used spelling, punctuation and grammar, and possibly signs of going back through the answer to make corrections.

ANSWERS

For your own notes

....
....
....
....
....
....
....
....
....
....
....
....
....
....
....
....
....
....
....
....
....
....
....
....
....
....
....
....
....

For your own notes

....
....
....

For your own notes

....
....
....
....
....
....
....
....
....
....
....
....
....
....
....
....
....
....
....
....
....
....
....
....
....
....
....
....
....
....
....
....

For your own notes

....
....
....

Published by Pearson Education Limited, 80 Strand, London, WC2R 0RL.

www.pearsonschoolsandfecolleges.co.uk

Copies of official specifications for all Pearson qualifications may be found on the website: qualifications.pearson.com

Text and illustrations © Pearson Education Ltd 2018
Typeset and illustrated by York Publishing Solutions Pvt Ltd, India.
Commissioning, editorial and project management services by Haremi Ltd.
Cover illustration by Miriam Sturdee

The right of Eileen Sagar to be identified as author of this work has been asserted by her in accordance with the
Copyright, Designs and Patents Act 1988.

First published 2018

2022
10 9 8 7 6 5 4 3 2

British Library Cataloguing in Publication Data
A catalogue record for this book is available from the British Library

ISBN 978 1 292 21372 9

Printed in Great Britain by Ashford Colour Press Ltd.

Acknowledgements
The author and publisher would like to thank the following individuals and organisations for permission to reproduce copyright material.
Page 006, 027, 038, 101: Reproduced with the permission of Associated Newspapers Ltd.
Page 019, 028, 037, 102: Reproduced with the permission of Bill Bryson.
Page 111, 112: Copyright Guardian News & Media Ltd 2017.
Page: 002, 029, 035, 038, 039, 105, 115: From I Am Malala: The Girl Who Stood Up for Education and Was Shot by the Taliban by Malala Yousafzai with Christina Lamb, Map by John Gikes. Copyright © 2015 by Salarzai Limited. Used by permission of Little, Brown books for Young Readers.
Page 014, 018, 025, 030, 104: Reproduced with the permission of The Nature Conservancy.
Page 015, 030, 039, 103: Reproduced with the permission of Times Internet Limited.
Page 015, 039, 103, 117, 121, 122: ©2006 By Doris S. Burville, Olympia, WA. USA. www.lettertoateenager.com

Photographs
(Key: b-bottom; c-centre; l-left; r-right; t-top)
123RF: Michael Shake 106tr, Vesilvio 106b, Jens Tandler 109t; **Alamy Stock Photo**: Hero Images Inc. 109b; **Shutterstock**: Ronsmith 106tl
All other images © Pearson Education

Notes from the publisher

1. While the publishers have made every attempt to ensure that advice on the qualification and its assessment is accurate, the official specification and associated assessment guidance materials are the only authoritative source of information and should always be referred to for definitive guidance.
Pearson examiners have not contributed to any sections in this resource relevant to examination papers for which they have responsibility.
2. Pearson has robust editorial processes, including answer and fact checks, to ensure the accuracy of the content in this publication, and every effort is made to ensure this publication is free of errors. We are, however, only human, and occasionally errors do occur. Pearson is not liable for any misunderstandings that arise as a result of errors in this publication, but it is our priority to ensure that the content is accurate. If you spot an error, please do contact us at resourcescorrections@pearson.com so we can make sure it is corrected.